Project AIR FORCE
RAND

OPERATIONS AGAINST ENEMY LEADERS

Stephen T. Hosmer

Prepared for the United States Air Force

Approved for public release; distribution unlimited

The research reported here was sponsored by the United States Air Force under Contract F49642-01-C-0003. Further information may be obtained from the Strategic Planning Division, Directorate of Plans, Hq USAF.

Library of Congress Cataloging-in-Publication Data

Hosmer, Stephen T.
    Operations against enemy leaders / Stephen T. Hosmer.
      p. cm.
    MR-1385
    Includes bibliographical references.
    ISBN 0-8330-3028-0
      1. Insurgency. 2. Coups d'âtat. 3. Assassination. 4. United States—Military policy. I. Title.

    JC328.5 .H67 2001
    327.1273—dc21

                                    2001041740

RAND is a nonprofit institution that helps improve policy and decisionmaking through research and analysis. RAND® is a registered trademark. RAND's publications do not necessarily reflect the opinions or policies of its research sponsors.

Cover design by Maritta Tapanainen

Published 2001 by RAND
1700 Main Street, P.O. Box 2138, Santa Monica, CA 90407-2138
1200 South Hayes Street, Arlington, VA 22202-5050
201 North Craig Street, Suite 102, Pittsburgh, PA 15213
RAND URL: http://www.rand.org/
To order RAND documents or to obtain additional information, contact Distribution Services: Telephone: (310) 451-7002;
Fax: (310) 451-6915; Email: order@rand.org

This report assesses the political-military efficacy of U.S. operations to remove senior enemy leaders. Three forms of leadership attacks are assessed: (1) operations that aim to directly attack the leader's person, (2) operations that are designed to foment and facilitate the leader's overthrow by an internal coup or rebellion, and (3) operations that aim to secure the leader's ouster through takedown by external military forces. Among other issues, the report examines the prerequisites of the effective use of U.S. air power in direct attacks and in support of coups, rebellions, and takedowns.

The report analyzes some 24 cases of leadership attack conducted or planned by the United States and other powers during the past 50 years. These past cases provide important insights about both the policy and the operational dimensions of leadership attacks, including

- the assumptions underlying the employment of leadership attacks and the conditions under which they are most likely to be sanctioned

- the comparative efficacy and prerequisites for success of different forms of attacks

- the potential deterrent and coercive value of leadership attacks for shaping future enemy policy and behavior

- the reasons leadership attacks frequently fail to produce the outcomes intended by the attackers.

The report is intended for the use of military and civilian officials concerned with the management, planning, and conduct of U.S.

operations to deter and counter threats to U.S. interests from enemy regimes, terrorist groups, and other hostile actors. The research for the report was completed in March 2001, well before the events of September 11, 2001. The basic points made here remain accurate and relevant.

The report is part of a larger RAND study, conducted within the Strategy and Doctrine Program of Project AIR FORCE, of the uses of air and space power in future conflicts that was sponsored by the Air Force Assistant Deputy Chief of Staff for Air and Space Operations and by the Air Force Director of Strategic Planning.

The primary objective of the overall study was to explore the prospects for developing a construct for air and space power that capitalizes on forthcoming air and space technologies and associated concepts of operation; that is effective against adversaries with diverse economies, cultures, political institutions, and military capabilities; and that offers an expansive concept of air and space power across the entire spectrum of conflict. Comments are welcome and may be addressed to the author or to the Strategy and Doctrine Program director, Edward R. Harshberger.

PROJECT AIR FORCE

Project AIR FORCE, a division of RAND, is the Air Force federally funded research and development center (FFRDC) for studies and analyses. It provides the Air Force with independent analyses of policy alternatives affecting the development, employment, combat readiness, and support of current and future aerospace forces. Research is carried out in four programs: Aerospace Force Development; Manpower, Personnel, and Training; Resource Management; and Strategy and Doctrine.

CONTENTS

TABLE

THE APPEAL AND FORMS OF SENIOR LEADERSHIP ATTACKS

Operations that threaten the person and power of senior enemy decisionmakers have long been considered to have a high payoff potential. They target a key enemy center of gravity and place at risk the individuals considered responsible for initiating and sustaining assaults on U.S. interests. Most important, they are thought to be a promising instrument for shortening wars, effecting other changes in enemy policy and behavior, and degrading enemy war-fighting capability.

Leadership attacks are seen to have significant deterrent and coercive value in that they threaten the things almost any enemy leader should value most: personal power and safety. Such attacks are also thought to send a message to other would-be malefactors about the types of punishment they might expect in the event that they were to harm U.S. interests.

The promise of such benefits has led U.S. civilian and military officials over the years to propose, sanction, and order attacks against senior enemy leaders. Three forms of attack have been used: direct attacks on the leader's person by U.S. forces or agents; coups and rebellions fomented and supported by the United States; and takedown operations conducted by U.S. invasion and occupation forces. Only the last form of attack has produced consistently successful results.

EFFECTS OF PAST LEADERSHIP ATTACKS

An analysis of some 24 cases of leadership attacks from World War II to the present provides insights about the comparative efficacy of different forms of leadership attacks, the potential coercive and deterrent value of such operations for shaping future enemy policy and behavior, and the possible unintended consequences that may result from the ill-considered use of such attacks.

Poor Results with Direct Attacks, Coups, and Rebellions

With the single exception of the shoot-down of Admiral Isoroku Yamamoto's aircraft in World War II, all U.S. operations to neutralize senior enemy leaders by direct attack have failed. The targets that have escaped elimination by aerial or other direct U.S. attack include Fidel Castro, Muammar al-Qaddafi, Saddam Hussein, Mohamed Farah Aideed, Osama bin Laden, and Slobodan Milosevic. These leaders proved difficult to neutralize because (1) they were routinely protected by elaborate security measures that denied attackers both access to their person and timely intelligence about their location; (2) they relocated to "safe houses" in civilian residential areas or to hardened facilities when threatened; and (3) self-imposed legal, political, and humanitarian constraints limited the means by which they could be attacked.

The United States has also had minimal success in securing the over-throw of regimes by coup d'état. The only coups explicitly sponsored or sanctioned by the United States that have succeeded have been against weakly entrenched governments: the Mossadeq regime in Iran and the Diem government in South Vietnam. In both instances, the coups were directed at regimes that enjoyed little support from their own military and were conducted by indigenous forces that had a close relationship with the United States. Coup attempts have failed when the targeted governments—such as those in Libya, Panama, and Iraq—have been protected by ubiquitous intelligence and internal security services, large praetorian guard forces, or other loyalist units. These coups either have died aborning—because they were infiltrated by government agents from the outset—or have been rapidly crushed by superior government forces.

America's attempts to oust enemy regimes by fomenting indigenous rebellions also have met with limited success. The one U.S. triumph—the ouster of the Arbenz regime in Guatemala—was accomplished by limited air attacks and ground force demonstrations against a government that was denied backing from its own military forces. All U.S. attempts to foster the overthrow of well-entrenched regimes have failed, either because the indigenous populations lacked the motivation and opportunity to rise up or because the rebels, when they did arise, lacked the military prowess to defeat superior progovernment forces.

Even Successful Attacks Often Have Not Produced Desired Results

The demise or incapacitation of an enemy leader often does not result in a favorable change in enemy policy or behavior. Belligerent states and nonstate organizations are often governed by a collective leadership or possess competent second-echelon leaders who are as strongly motivated to continue a struggle as was the fallen leader. The frequent futility of leadership attacks is borne out by the experience of Israel in its attempts to suppress Palestinian terrorism and Russia in its attempts to pacify Chechnya. Indeed, analyses of the effects of political assassinations from antiquity through modern times document the infrequency with which the killing of a particular leader has produced the results hoped for by the assassin.

Some Attacks Have Risked or Produced Counterproductive Results

Experience also shows that leadership attacks can produce extremely harmful unintended consequences. Had U.S. bombing of the Imperial Palace in Tokyo, as was proposed in World War II, killed Emperor Hirohito, Japan's surrender might have been significantly delayed at the cost of many additional American lives. The French hijacking of the Front de Libération Nationale leader Ahmed Ben Bella during the Algerian war proved to be a major blunder as it increased the militancy of both the front and its external-state supporters. The U.S. helicopter gunship attack on Somali National Alliance leaders in Mogadishu on July 12, 1993, also proved to be a major error in that it dramatically increased support for General Aideed and generated such strong anti-American sentiments that Somalis were thereafter motivated to kill U.S. troops.

The Threat of Direct Attacks and Coups Has Had Limited Coercive and Deterrent Effect

The prospect that the United States might mount a direct attack on a leader or attempt to foment and support his overthrow by a coup seems to have had little deterrent or coercive effect on enemy leaders. Castro, Qaddafi, Noriega, Saddam, and bin Laden all continued to pursue policies that were anathema to the United States after being targeted by such U.S. operations. None capitulated to U.S. demands even after what appeared to be narrow escapes from direct U.S. attacks.

Several factors seem to explain this defiant behavior. First, the leaders apparently believed that their security measures would allow them to successfully evade or defeat any future attacks on their person or power. Second, some of the targeted leaders also apparently believed that their acquiescence to the policy and behavior changes demanded by the United States might severely undermine their credibility and authority among the key constituencies that maintained them in power. Finally, some leaders were apparently sufficiently committed to their cause that they were willing to die for it.

Experience also suggests, however, that there may be circumstances in which an enemy leader will find it preferable to accept allied terms for war termination rather than run the risk that continued allied bombing might eventually spark a domestic upheaval sufficient to produce his overthrow. Some enemy leaders may be paranoid about the internal threats to their regime and may overestimate the potential danger caused by U.S. air operations. As a result, air operations might at times provide greater negotiating leverage than they actually merit.

Support for Rebellions Sometimes Produced Coercive Leverage

While not always fruitful, U.S. support for rebellions and resistance movements produced useful coercive leverage in several conflict situations. The covert support provided to the National Union for the Total Independence of Angola (UNITA) and to the Mujaheddin in Afghanistan helped prompt the withdrawal of external communist military forces from those countries. The covert assistance the

United States rendered to the Contras helped persuade the Sandinista regime in Nicaragua to terminate its arms transfers to the Salvadoran guerrillas and to hold democratic elections.

These successful U.S. operations shared several commonalities. In each instance, the United States (1) backed resistance movements that were able to recruit large numbers of motivated fighters; (2) enjoyed access to proximate base areas from which to mount its support operations; (3) was able to sustain its support over a protracted period; and (4) pursued political-military objectives that fell short of seeking the military overthrow of the incumbent enemy regime. The targeted regimes obviously saw things differently, however, perceiving any U.S. military support to their opponents as ultimately designed to secure their ouster. Finally, the United States augmented the bargaining leverage derived from its support of the resistance movements with broader packages of economic and diplomatic sanctions and incentives aimed at encouraging enemy acquiescence.

External Takedowns Produced More Certain and Lasting Results

The surest way to unseat a hostile regime is to oust it with external military force. Since the takedown of the Axis powers in World War II, the United States has invaded and occupied three states to remove enemy regimes: Grenada in 1983, Panama in 1989, and Haiti in 1994. In each instance, the United States disestablished the military and security services that had maintained the previous regimes in power and promoted elections to select new governing bodies and national leadership. Thus, the effect of a takedown on a targeted country's policy and behavior is likely to be more fundamental and lasting than is the effect secured by the elimination of a single head of state or by a coup d'état against a particular government.

The Threat of a Takedown Can Have Deterrent and Coercive Effects

For an enemy leader, the threat of overthrow and punishment by external military force may also have a greater deterrent and coercive effect than the threat of death or removal by direct attack or coup.

Whereas a leader may believe that he can evade or defeat these latter threats, the prospects for fending off a U.S. invasion would probably be viewed as quite another matter so long as the enemy leader believed that the United States possessed the political will and freedom of action to actually take down his regime. This seemed to be the case with Saddam during the Gulf War, when the threat of a possible Coalition march on Baghdad apparently prompted the Iraqi leader to instantly accept all Coalition demands at the Safwan cease-fire negotiations and helped deter him from using weapons of mass destruction in that conflict.

IMPLICATIONS FOR THE DESIGN AND CONDUCT OF FUTURE LEADERSHIP ATTACKS

The historical analysis also provides insights about the likely conditions under which future leadership attacks might be sanctioned and the prerequisites of the effective use of air power in direct attacks and in support of coups, rebellions, and takedowns.

Potential Consequences Must Be Carefully Weighed

As with the physician, the decisionmaker's first concern in leadership attack should be to do no harm. Because such attacks can prove counterproductive, U.S. decisionmakers must be confident that the possible short- and long-term benefits of an attack will outweigh its possible costs. To make such assessments, decisionmakers should consult knowledgeable area experts to determine the likely reactions of enemy and other publics to a successful leadership attack, its possible impact on power relationships within the enemy camp, and how it is likely to affect the enemy policy and behavior that the United States wishes to modify. Particular importance should be attached to establishing the identification and probable policy orientation of the targeted leader's likely successor.

Situations Where Direct Attacks Are Likely to Be Sanctioned

The experience to date suggests that U.S. decisionmakers may be willing to sanction direct military attacks against enemy heads of state so long as the attacks can be

- justified under the right of self-defense as protecting important U.S. national interests

- said to be directed against enemy facilities that serve a military or security function, such as command and control

- conducted by uniformed members of the armed services in accordance with the law of armed conflict

- embedded in a larger military campaign in which other targets are being attacked as well.

Decisionmakers will be most willing to sanction leadership attacks when they believe the targeted leader is the key promoter or facilitator of the policy and behavior that the United States desires to change.

However, except in cases of notorious terrorists, such as Osama bin Laden, decisionmakers will continue to be loath to publicly concede that a specific enemy leader is the actual target of a U.S. attack. They will be particularly reluctant to sanction attacks that might appear to violate Executive Order 12333 prohibiting U.S. involvement in assassinations, such as employment of ruses to lure leaders to sites where they will be vulnerable to attack.

Prerequisites of Effective Air Attacks on Enemy Leaders

Because enemy leaders frequently change location to foil assassination plots and other threats, the success of any air attack will depend importantly on the availability of accurate, near-real-time or predictive intelligence about the leader's location and movements. Since U.S. forces must be capable of striking the target within the window provided by this intelligence, predictive intelligence will be essential if significant time is needed to mount an attack.

Special munitions may be required to successfully attack some leadership targets. In the event of another Korean conflict, for example, a large inventory of penetrating weapons would be needed to attack the numerous leadership and command, control, and communications sites that are located deep underground throughout North Korea. In situations where enemy leaders seek refuge from attack by relocating to civilian residential areas, accurate low-yield munitions will be required to attack such sites without causing unacceptable civilian casualties.

Air Support to Coups and Rebellions

On its own, U.S. air intervention can neither negate many of the strengths that maintain a regime in power nor compensate for the fundamental deficiencies of the groups seeking its ouster. Under the right conditions, however, U.S. air power could enhance the prospects of a coup or rebellion. American air strikes conducted prior to the outbreak of active opposition could help stimulate a coup or rebellion and, if the attacks on the regime's security apparatus were sufficiently accurate, sustained, and intense, might even significantly weaken the regime's defenses against overthrow.

However, it is direct U.S. air support that holds the greatest potential for increasing the ultimate military success of coup and rebel forces. The very prospect of U.S. air support might embolden otherwise quiescent elements to move against the government, and the appearance of such support during an actual coup or rebellion might encourage some otherwise proregime forces to remain neutral or even to take up arms against the government. Along with such psychological effects, U.S. air intervention could also decisively tip the battlefield balance of power between opposition and regime forces.

Prerequisites of Effective Air Support to Coups. The key tasks that U.S. air power might perform in support of a coup include denying air support to regime forces; degrading regime command, control, and communications; interdicting regime armored and artillery forces; and providing close air support to embattled coup forces. Such U.S. air support is unlikely to be sanctioned or prove effective unless U.S. forces were (1) permitted to act overtly, which would constitute a major departure from past U.S. practice; (2) capable of establishing immediate communication with coup leaders to coordinate operations and avert fratricide; and (3) postured and prepared to intervene promptly.

Because the outcome of most coups is likely to be decided within hours rather than days, U.S. air units must be ready and able to respond on short notice. This will require prior agreement—both within the U.S. government and with the host nations from whose territory U.S. operations would be mounted—about the actions U.S. forces might take in the event of a decision to support a coup. In the likely event that the United States had no forewarning of a coup, U.S. decisionmakers must be prepared to render a rapid judgment about whether the coup appeared to have sufficient military and political prospect to merit a U.S. involvement.

Prerequisites of Effective Air Support to Rebellions. Historically, rebellions have involved a wide spectrum of dissident activity ranging from the spontaneous and sudden popular uprisings that sometimes engulf discredited regimes to the protracted insurrections that are often conducted by alienated ethnic, religious, and political groups. To seize power, rebellions of all stripes must achieve a common end state: They must accumulate sufficient popular support and military force to defeat or subvert the military and security elements that maintain the regime's rule.

To oust a regime protected by numerous well-armed loyalist units, insurgents must be able to expand their forces and progressively move to higher levels of warfare. The transition from guerrilla and small-unit operations to mobile warfare typically requires extensive external arms, training, and logistical support. External air intervention could further facilitate and accelerate this transition by helping protect rebel forces when they are most vulnerable during the early defensive phase of their operations and by providing them with potent firepower when they later go on to the offensive. The specific tasks that might be performed by U.S. air elements in support of a rebellion include the full panoply of support operations typically provided U.S. ground forces.

For U.S. air support to help propel a rebel movement to victory, the following conditions would likely be required. First and foremost, the rebellion must possess sufficient cohesion, discipline, and popular appeal to eventually generate the troop strengths needed to effectively challenge government forces. Second, the terrain in which the rebels will initially operate must provide sufficient cover for small-unit operations. Third, proximate bases must be available for the equipping, training, and resupply of rebel forces and for the conduct of U.S. air operations. Fourth, U.S. forces must be willing to operate overtly. Fifth, since it may take years for an opposition group to gather sufficient strength to mount a successful overthrow, there must be sufficient popular support—both within the United States and within the host nations providing bases—to sustain a protracted U.S. involvement. Finally, the United States must be prepared to escalate its military involvement in the event that its rebel clients or host-nation allies come under severe attack.

Air Support to Takedowns

Decisionmakers will be reluctant to sanction the invasion and occupation of an enemy state because of the potential political, financial, and human costs that might be incurred by such action. They will be particularly cautious about signing on to takedown operations that might entail significant U.S. casualties and protracted U.S. combat involvements. It is worth noting that all of America's post–World War II takedowns were targeted against governments that possessed extremely weak military forces that could be overwhelmed rapidly with little U.S. loss of life. Even so, the takedowns in Panama and Haiti were operations of last resort that were undertaken after other options for removing the regimes in those countries had been tried and had failed.

Prerequisites of Air Support to Takedowns. One can conceive of future circumstances in which U.S. decisionmakers might find it necessary to threaten or order the takedown of an enemy state possessing even sizable, well-equipped military forces. The precipitating events that might provoke such action would include situations where a hostile regime (1) caused or threatened to cause large numbers of U.S. military or civilian casualties by employing weapons of mass destruction; (2) sponsored or abetted repeated terrorist attacks against U.S. citizens and facilities; and (3) repeated a major act of aggression that the United States had previously helped repulse.

Since the minimization of U.S. casualties may be essential for sustaining public support for such takedowns, U.S. air elements will require the capability to gain air supremacy and prepare the battlefield so that any organized opposition to the invasion and occupation will be limited and short lived. This will require that U.S. forces have access to proximate bases or robust long-range strike capabilities and possess sufficient aircraft, missiles, and munitions to progressively degrade both the enemy's physical combat capability and his will to fight. In addition, U.S. forces will require the capability to provide necessary airlift, interdiction, and close support to attacking ground troops. Because they may require robust forces, potential takedowns should be included among the major contingencies that size U.S. force postures.

ACKNOWLEDGMENTS

The author is indebted to Alexander L. George and Paul B. Henze for their careful reviews of the manuscript and for their thoughtful comments and suggestions.

ABBREVIATIONS

ARVN	Army of Vietnam
C^3	Command, control, and communications
C^3I	Command, control, communications, and intelligence
CENTCOM	U.S. Central Command
CIA	Central Intelligence Agency
FLN	Front de Libération Nationale
FNLA	National Liberation Front of Angola
FRY	Federal Republic of Yugoslavia
HUMINT	Human intelligence
INC	Iraqi National Congress
JCS	Joint Chiefs of Staff
KLA	Kosovo Liberation Army
KPNLF	Kampuchea/Khmer People's National Liberation Front
KTO	Kuwait Theater of Operations
MPLA	Popular Movement for the Liberation of Angola
NATO	North Atlantic Treaty Organization
PDF	Panama Defense Force

PKK	Kurdish Workers' Party
PSYOP	Psychological operations
SNA	Somali National Alliance
SOE	Special Operations Executive
SOUTHCOM	U.S. Southern Command
UN	United Nations
UNITA	National Union for the Total Independence of Angola
UNOSOM	UN Operation in Somalia
UNSCOM	UN Special Commission
WIN	Freedom and Independence Movement
WMD	Weapons of mass destruction

Chapter One

INTRODUCTION

OBJECTIVES OF LEADERSHIP ATTACKS

The United States has long attempted to use leadership attacks to shape the policy and behavior of enemy states and other hostile actors. Over the years, both overt and covert operations have been mounted in attempts to kill enemy leaders directly or to secure their overthrow either by indigenous coup or rebellion or by external invasion. Through such attacks, the United States has variously sought to (1) compel enemy states to abandon policies and behavior injurious to American interests, (2) deter adversaries from making future assaults on those interests, (3) depose potentially dangerous regimes, and (4) degrade enemy capabilities to wage war and engage in terrorism.[1]

---

[1]While not the focus of this study, it is important to note that the United States has also frequently employed nonviolent means to shape the policy and behavior of enemy states and to encourage and facilitate the ouster of regimes whose foreign or domestic behavior was considered inimical to U.S. interests and values. These measures have often served as corollaries to the violent operations that the United States has mounted and supported to remove enemy leaders and governments. Among other actions, the United States has sought to coerce, weaken, and stimulate domestic opposition to hostile and repressive regimes by (1) withdrawing or threatening to withdraw U.S. recognition and support, (2) promoting the imposition of trade sanctions and arms embargoes, (3) acting to deny credits from international lending institutions, (4) fostering condemnation and isolation in international forums, (5) disseminating antiregime information to indigenous domestic audiences, and (6) when circumstances have permitted, providing political, financial, and other nonmilitary aid to indigenous opponents. As an incentive to regime opponents, the United States has also held out the promise of early recognition, economic and military assistance, and reintegration into the international community once the offending regime was removed. While such pressures and inducements by themselves have generally proved insufficient to bring down hostile heads of state, they have on occasion con-

Compel Changes in Enemy Policy and Behavior

One of the most ambitious objectives of past leadership attacks has been to cause a hostile actor already engaged in military aggression or terrorism to cease such activity and accede to other demands posed by the United States and its allies. The 1986 air attack on Muammar al-Qaddafi's residence in Tripoli aimed to persuade the Libyan leader to cease his use and sponsorship of terrorism. The attacks on leadership-related targets in Iraq were directed first at inducing Saddam Hussein to withdraw from Kuwait and later at encouraging him to permit unfettered UN Special Commission (UNSCOM) inspections of possible Iraqi weapons of mass destruction (WMD) sites. The 1999 NATO air attacks on Milosevic's various residencies in Serbia were part of a broader air effort to persuade him to accept NATO's terms for a resolution of the crisis in Kosovo.

Leadership attacks provide several potential mechanisms for bringing about policy change in an enemy state. First, the hostile leader advocating the policy and behavior that the United States finds abhorrent may be eliminated or incapacitated and replaced by a successor whose policy orientation may be more compatible with U.S. interests. Second, the targeted leader may find the prospect of U.S.

---

tributed to the downfall of leaders the United States wished to see removed. In the case of Slobodan Milosevic, for example, the continued economic hardships imposed on the Federal Republic of Yugoslavia by international sanctions and loan denials and the prospect that these penalties would remain in place so long as Milosevic held power undoubtedly contributed to the former Federal Republic of Yugoslavia president's electoral defeat on September 24, 2000. It is also probable that the financial and other aid the United States provided to the Yugoslav opposition political parties, the independent media, and the youth protest movement *Otpor* ("Resistance") also played a role in opposition candidate Vojislav Kostunica's victory. However, other factors appear to have been more decisive to Milosevic's electoral defeat: His years of rule had produced a "succession of lost wars, hundreds of thousands of Serbs uprooted, an economy ruined, [and] wages slashed," and a region once considered relatively prosperous "turned into a conspicuous center of poverty." (Roger Cohen, "After the Lost Wars and the Ruined Economy, 'the Greater Slobo' Falls Silent," *New York Times*, October 6, 2000a, p. A14.) The Federal Republic of Yugoslavia's economic decline was greatly intensified by the North Atlantic Treaty Organization (NATO) bombing, and the loss of Serb control over Kosovo severely undercut Milosevic's stature as a statesman and nationalist leader. Finally, in a departure from previous national elections, Milosevic confronted a largely united opposition that funneled most anti-Milosevic votes to Kostunica. See R. Jeffrey Smith and Peter Finn, "How Milosevic Lost His Grip," *Washington Post*, October 15, 2000, pp. A1, A30; David E. Sanger, "The Plan: He Steps Down, They Step Up, U.S. Lies Low," *New York Times*, October 6, 2000, p. A15, and Roger Cohen, "Who Really Brought Down Milosevic?" *New York Times Magazine*, November 26, 2000b, pp. 43–47, 118, 148.

attacks on his person and power to be so threatening that he will accede to U.S. demands to ward off future attacks. Third, the elimination of a leader may engender a succession struggle or other division within the enemy camp and force the successor leadership to seek a respite from conflict and agree to a settlement acceptable to the United States.

Deter Assaults on U.S. Interests

Deterrence has been another major objective of U.S. leadership attacks. Washington decisionmakers have sought to send a "signal" both to the targeted leader and to other would-be aggressors that the United States would impose a heavy cost in the event that other assaults were made against U.S. interests. This type of generic signaling was part of the rationale for the U.S. air attacks on Qaddafi and on General Mohammed Farah Aideed and the other Somali National Alliance (SNA) leaders in Mogadishu. Washington's desire to demonstrate that terrorists "have no place to hide" was also a motivating factor in the U.S. cruise missile attack on Osama bin Laden in Afghanistan.

Depose Potentially Dangerous Regimes

Occasionally, U.S. decisionmakers have concluded that a regime posed a sufficient threat to U.S. national interests that it merited overthrow. During the Cold War, concerns about expanding communist lodgments in the Third World led the United States to seek the ouster of governments deemed already committed to Moscow or likely to fall within the Soviet orbit. This was the rationale underlying the U.S. Central Intelligence Agency (CIA)–supported overthrows during the Eisenhower administration of the Mossadeq regime in Iran and the Arbenz government in Guatemala. It also underlay the Kennedy administration's abortive attempts to oust the Castro regime in Cuba. More recently, in the post–Cold War era, Clinton administration officials publicly called for Saddam Hussein's and Slobodan Milosevic's removal from power.

Degrade Enemy Capabilities

An objective present in most leadership attacks is to degrade the enemy's capability to wage war or mount terrorist operations. In wartime, attacks on enemy leaders and their command, control, and communications (C^3) facilities aim to reduce the enemy leader's ability to see the battlefield, maneuver his forces, and react promptly to friendly threats. Such attacks often force enemy leaders to disperse to alternative command sites, which may degrade their communications and make them more vulnerable to friendly intercept. The killing or disabling of enemy leaders may also diminish the quality of the enemy's command and control by conferring command on less competent personnel. Finally, the loss of leaders may serve to demoralize enemy military forces and civilian populations.

STUDY APPROACH

The scope and focus of the research documented in this report differs significantly from the earlier literature relating to leadership attacks. Whereas previous works have concentrated on a single form of leadership attack (e.g., coups in Latin America), a particular U.S. or foreign operation, or a set of U.S. covert activities over a limited time frame, this report systematically examines and evaluates the entire spectrum of violent leadership attacks that the United States has mounted or supported during the past half century. Again, in contrast to most earlier works, the report seeks to distill from this historical experience policy and operational lessons that should help guide U.S. decisionmakers and military commanders contemplating the use of such attacks in the future.

The study assesses the political-military efficacy of leadership attacks aimed at three of the objectives discussed above: the coercion, deterrence, and ousting of enemy regimes. Three basic concepts of operation for conducting such leadership attacks are examined. These are to cause or threaten to cause a leader's removal by

- conducting a direct attack on his person
- facilitating a coup or rebellion against his continued rule
- using external military force to take down his regime.

To gain insight into the potential efficacy of these concepts of operation, the author examined 24 cases of past leadership attack (see Table 1.1). Included in these cases were the principal leadership attacks conducted by the United States since World War II and sev-

Table 1.1

Cases of Proposed or Executed Past Leadership Attacks Examined

Target	Attack Directly	Foster Coup	Foster Rebellion	Take Down by Invasion
Yamamoto (1943, Bougainville)	X			
Mussolini (1943, Italy)		X	X	
Hitler (1944, Germany)	X			
Hirohito (1945, Japan)	X			
Hoxa (1950s, Albania)			X	
Mossadeq (1953, Iran)		X		
Arbenz (1954, Guatemala)			X	
Ben Bella (1956, Algeria)	X			
Sukarno (1956–1958, Indonesia)			X	
Castro (1960s, Cuba)	X	X	X	
Diem (1963, South Vietnam)		X		
Palestinian terrorists (1967–2001, Mideast)	X			
Kabul regime/Soviets (1980s, Afghanistan)			X	
Dos Santos (1980–1981, Angola)			X	
Hudson Austin (1983, Grenada)				X
Qaddafi (1986, Libya)	X	X		
Sandinistas (1980s, Nicaragua)			X	
Noriega (1989, Panama)		X		X
Saddam (1991–1999, Iraq)	X	X	X	
Aideed/SNA (1993, Somalia)	X			
Cedras (1994, Haiti)				X
Dudayev (1996, Chechnya)	X			X
Osama bin Laden (1998, Afghanistan)	X			
Milosevic (1999, Serbia)	X	X	X	

eral of the most prominent cases of leadership attack conducted by foreign powers. Because they illustrate some of the potential pitfalls of leadership attack, the author also assessed several leadership attacks that were proposed or planned by U.S. or allied officials but never actually executed.

In addition to the cases arrayed in Table 1.1, the author also examined operations where the United States supported rebel groups for purposes other than leadership removal. Finally, the author surveyed the literature regarding political assassinations for the insights it might provide about the policy effects of leadership attacks.

SOURCES

Leadership attacks typically fall in the domain of covert or otherwise closely held operations, and governments are reluctant to openly admit, much less provide evidence of, their involvement in such operations. Such inhibitions, however, tend to erode with the passage of time, and a substantial body of credible information concerning the cases examined in this report is now available in the open literature.

Among other sources, the author has been able to draw upon recently declassified official histories and critiques of past U.S. and U.K. covert operations; the memoirs and statements of U.S. civilian and military officials who directly participated in the oversight, management, planning, or conduct of U.S. operations to remove enemy leaders or who were conversant with policy discussions relating to proposed operations; congressional assessments of U.S. involvement in attempted assassinations and other leadership attacks; and histories and other documented analyses of particular types and cases of leadership attack. Journalistic accounts have also provided credible source materials when such accounts have been informed by interviews with government officials or other persons who were knowledgeable about the conduct and effects of the leadership attacks under discussion.

While the physical success or failure of a particular leadership attack can usually be easily demonstrated, it is more difficult to document the possible psychological effects of an attack, such as whether an attack so frightened an enemy leader that it made him more prone to compromise. Except for the instances where we have testimony about the presence or absence of such psychological effects from credible sources close to the targeted leader, conclusions about the possible intimidatory or deterrent effects of a particular leadership attack must be inferred from an analysis of the enemy leader's subsequent behavior.

ORGANIZATION OF THE REPORT

The following chapters analyze the three concepts of operation for leadership attack: attacking the leader directly (Chapter Two), facilitating coups or rebellions (Chapter Three), and taking down regimes with external military force (Chapter Four). Each concept of operation is examined in terms of the assumptions likely to underlie its adoption, the constraints that may circumscribe its employment, its past effectiveness in securing intended objectives, and its potential coercive and deterrent value for shaping enemy policy and behavior. The potential contributions and prerequisites of the effective use of air power in each of these concepts of operation are also examined.

The report concludes with brief summary observations (Chapter Five) about the comparative efficacy of different concepts of operation, the circumstance under which attacks are most likely to be sanctioned, the prerequisites of the effective use of air power, and the deterrent and coercive effects of threats to remove leaders.

Chapter Two

ATTACKING LEADERS DIRECTLY

ASSUMPTIONS UNDERLYING DIRECT ATTACKS

Any decision to conduct a direct attack on an enemy leader is likely to be predicated on several key assumptions. In sanctioning such action, the decisionmaker will expect the attack to

- conform to existing moral, legal, and political constraints

- stand a reasonable chance of producing the physical, coercive, or deterrent effect desired

- produce no harmful, unintended consequences.

The experiential data on direct leadership attacks accumulated to date suggest that the decisionmaker would be well advised to approach the last two of these assumptions with considerable skepticism. Indeed, experience shows that direct leadership attacks are usually unsuccessful and, even when successful, rarely produce the effects intended. Moreover, some leadership attacks can be catastrophically counterproductive.

CONSTRAINTS ON LEADERSHIP ATTACKS

Leadership attacks must adhere to the same moral, legal, and political constraints that circumscribe other U.S. military operations. The attacks must not violate the law of armed conflict or the principles of necessity, proportion, and discrimination that underlie the concept of a just war. Particular caution must be exercised to minimize injury to innocent noncombatants and to avoid other unnecessary collateral damage.[1]

Care must also be taken to avoid military actions that might alienate the American public and thereby undermine U.S. domestic support for a continued U.S. military involvement. In addition, decisionmakers must remain sensitive to the need to maintain some minimum of international support for U.S. military involvement, particularly among the populations and governments of states that provide bases and overflight rights for U.S. military operations.[2]

Each of these concerns may to some extent or other influence U.S. decisions about leadership attack. However, the constraint that will shape all such decisions will be the consistency of the proposed leadership attack with Executive Order 12333.

Executive Order 12333 Prohibiting Assassinations

Executive Order 12333, which pertains to U.S. intelligence activities, contains provisions that limit the U.S. government's freedom of action to directly or indirectly promote attacks on enemy leaders or support their overthrow. Following congressional hearings about U.S. involvement in assassination plots against officials in the Congo, Cuba, and the Dominican Republic in the 1960s and in Chile in the early 1970s, President Ford—possibly to preempt legislation on the subject—issued Executive Order 11905 in 1976, which contained provisions designed to assure Congress and the U.S. public that such practices would not be repeated. The prohibitive provisions contained in President Ford's executive order were reissued without significant change by subsequent U.S. presidents and are now embodied in Executive Order 12333 as follows:

> 2.11   Prohibition on Assassination. No person employed by or acting on behalf of the United States Government shall engage in, or conspire to engage in, assassination.

---

[1]For the law of armed conflict as it applies to air operations, see U.S. Department of the Air Force, *International Law: The Conduct of Armed Conflict and Air Operations*, AFP 110-31, Washington, D.C.: November 19, 1976. See also William V. O'Brien, *The Conduct of Just and Limited War*, New York: Praeger, 1981.

[2]Stephen T. Hosmer, *Constraints on U.S. Strategy in Third World Conflicts*, New York: Crane Russak & Company, 1987, p. 57.

2.12   Indirect Participation. No agency of the Intelligence Community shall participate in or request any person to undertake activities forbidden by this order.[3]

Over the years, commentators have disagreed about the scope of the executive order's prohibition. These arguments have risen in the main because the executive order provides no elucidation on what constitutes an assassination. Some believe that the order should be interpreted broadly as preventing the U.S. government "from directing, facilitating, encouraging, or even incidentally causing the killing of any specified individual, whatever the circumstances."[4] Other commentators view the prohibition more narrowly and see a distinction between operations in peacetime and operations in times of conflict, as well as between operations conducted covertly by intelligence personnel and operations conducted by U.S. military personnel. They see the executive order as barring only activities similar to the U.S. assassination attempts that gave rise to its issuance: peacetime efforts by U.S. intelligence officials to cause the death of targeted foreign persons, whose political activities are judged to be detrimental to U.S. security and foreign policy objectives.[5]

These commentators see a major distinction between intelligence operations aimed at assassination and military operations aimed at killing specific enemy combatants—including enemy leaders such as Saddam Hussein and Colonel Qaddafi—in situations where the United States is exercising its inherent right of self-defense.[6] According to W. Hays Parks, the United States generally recognizes three forms of self-defense: (1) "against an actual use of force, or hostile act," (2) "preemptive self-defense against an imminent use of force," and (3) "self-defense against a continuing threat."[7]

---

[3]Quoted in LCDR Patricia Zengel, "Assassination and the Law of Armed Conflict," *Military Law Review,* Fall 1991, pp. 144–145.

[4]Zengel (1991), pp. 145–146.

[5]Zengel (1991), p. 145.

[6]Zengel (1991), pp. 147–151.

[7]Parks argues that "a decision by the president to employ clandestine, low visibility, or overt military force would not constitute assassination if U.S. military forces were employed against the combatant forces of another nation, a guerrilla force, or a terrorist or other organization whose actions pose a threat to the security of the United States." (W. Hays Parks, "Memorandum of Law: Executive Order 12333 and Assassi-

Executive Order 12333 in Practice

Covert Attacks Have Been Constrained. In addition to preventing U.S.-initiated assassinations, Executive Order 12333 has restricted U.S. involvement with foreign elements planning attacks or coups against leaders hostile to the United States. Members of the clandestine services have been barred from supporting any groups contemplating the killing of leaders and have been instructed to dissuade dissident groups from taking such action whenever possible.

For a period up to the late 1980s, senior U.S. officials apparently even prohibited the provision of U.S. assistance to any attack or coup by indigenous forces that might lead to the death of a country's leader in the heat of battle. Thus, even though it was U.S. policy to actively encourage the overthrow of Manuel Noriega, CIA personnel were apparently barred from providing advice to dissident Panamanian officers who were plotting a coup in October 1989 because of the possibility that the coup might lead to Noriega's death.[8] The Reagan administration reportedly had reached an agreement with the Senate Intelligence Committee in 1988 that American officials would not become involved in Panama with coup plotters whose efforts could result in the assassination of Noriega.[9] This interpretation of Executive Order 12333 was reportedly overturned in late 1989 by a Justice Department legal opinion that held that

> the prohibition against supporting coup plotters applied only where assassination was the goal. . . . Additionally, the opinion made clear that Executive Order 12333 imposed no requirement to notify possible targets of coup plots.[10]

---

nation," *Army Lawyer*, December 1989, p. 7.) Parks wrote the memorandum while serving as chief of the International Law Branch, International Affairs Division, Judge Advocate General, U.S. Army.

[8]Stephen Engelberg, "C.I.A. Seeks Looser Rules on Killings During Coups," *New York Times*, October 17, 1989a, p. A8.

[9]It was further agreed that, should the CIA officials discover that Panamanians working with the United States were planning to kill Noriega, the officials would move to prevent it. See Stephen Engelberg, "Reagan Agreed to Prevent Noriega Death," *New York Times*, October 23, 1989b, p. A10.

[10]Michael N. Schmitt, "State-Sponsored Assassination in International and Domestic Law," *Yale Journal of International Law*, Vol. 17, Summer 1992, pp. 672–673, and Engleberg (1989a), p. A1.

However, the prohibition against U.S. involvement with indigenous plots to kill leaders remained. When a CIA officer working with the Kurdish resistance in northern Iraq in 1995 reported that resistance forces had learned from a former Iraqi general that a certain road traveled by Saddam Hussein was vulnerable to ambush, officials at CIA headquarters in Langley, Virginia, ordered the officer to discourage the resistance fighters from even attempting such an attack.[11] Resistance forces encountering such U.S. restrictions no doubt must have wondered how they were to oust a tyrant as well-protected and ruthless as Saddam Hussein without causing risk to his life and limb.

Overt Military Attacks Have Been Permitted. In contrast to the restrictions it has imposed on covert operations, Executive Order 12333 has not prevented concerted, overt U.S. military attacks against facilities that were suspected of holding senior enemy leaders. Indeed, the executive order's prohibitions on assassination did not prevent: (1) the bombing of Qaddafi's home and headquarters in the Azziziyah Barracks compound during the 1986 U.S. raid on Libya; (2) the air attacks mounted during the 1991 Gulf War on the various presidential residences and command-and-control bunkers known or suspected to be used by Saddam Hussein; (3) the U.S. helicopter gunship raid of July 12, 1993, on the SNA command-and-control center in Mogadishu, Somalia, which was thought to house high-level SNA leaders, possibly including Aideed himself; (4) the 1998 cruise missile strikes against the military site in Afghanistan expected to be occupied by the terrorist leader Osama bin Laden; or (5) the 1999 NATO air attacks against Slobodan Milosevic's residences and bunkers in Serbia during Operation Allied Force.

However, U.S. leaders refused to identify Qaddafi, Saddam, Aideed, or Milosevic as the actual targets of these attacks.[12] Instead, officials

---

[11]According to *Newsweek*, the CIA officer and the colleagues who served with him in the field were later investigated by the Federal Bureau of Investigation, which had picked up rumors that they had encouraged an illegal assassination plot. The investigation reportedly "went nowhere," and the CIA officer was decorated for his work in Iraq. See Evan Thomas, Christopher Dickey, and Gregory L. Vistica, "Bay of Pigs Redux," *Newsweek*, March 23, 1998, pp. 43–44.

[12]Clinton administration officials initially asserted that the 1998 U.S. cruise missile attacks on Afghanistan following the bombings of the U.S. embassies in Nairobi and Dar es Salaam had targeted only training facilities and not specific individuals. Administration officials said that the timing of the attack was dictated by intelligence

described the attacks as attempts to destroy headquarters sites, command-and-control centers, and terrorist facilities.

In a television address to the nation about the raid on Libya, President Reagan categorized the targets as "headquarters, terrorist facilities, and military assets" that supported Qaddafi's subversive activities.[13] During the planning of the raid, Qaddafi's residence had been selected as a target over the objections of U.S. Secretary of State George Shultz who had argued that the air strikes "wouldn't get him" and "would be seen as an attempt by us to kill him that failed."[14]

Even though he likened Saddam Hussein to Hitler and eventually openly called for his removal from power, President George Bush refused to allow the Iraqi leader's death to become a formal objective of the Coalition air campaign. Other senior American leaders also held the view that Saddam should not be made an explicit target. These military officers and civilian officials worried that making Saddam an objective might contravene Executive Order 12333. There was also a concern that the task of killing Saddam would prove too difficult and that if the Iraqi leader were made a formal target, the United States would be subject to an embarrassment similar to the one experienced during the prolonged hunt for General Noriega in Panama. Finally, U.S. leaders worried that the formal establishment of such an objective might require "complex and possibly counterproductive negotiations" with other powers, as a declared intent to eliminate Saddam would exceed the war aims agreed to in the various UN Security Council resolutions regarding Iraq.[15]

---

that a meeting of terrorist leaders was to be held at the sites—and press reports about the attack indicated that the attendees were to include Osama bin Laden. Later, administration officials admitted that bin Laden was indeed the prime target of the attack. See William Cohen, Statement on CNN, August 21, 1998.

[13]George P. Shultz, *Turmoil and Triumph*, New York: Charles Scribner's Sons, 1993, p. 686.

[14]Shultz (1993), p. 683.

[15]Thomas A. Keaney and Eliot A. Cohen, *Gulf War Air Power Survey: Summary Report*, Washington, D.C.: U.S. Government Printing Office, 1993, pp. 45–46; Barry D. Watts et al. *Gulf War Air Power Survey (GWAPS)*, Vol. II: *Operations and Effects and Effectiveness*, Part II: *Effects and Effectiveness*, Washington, D.C.: U.S. Government Printing Office, 1993b, pp. 76–77, 277; and Stephen T. Hosmer, *Psychological Effects of U.S. Air Operations in Four Wars 1941–1991: Lessons for U.S. Commanders*, Santa Monica, Calif.: RAND, MR-576-AF, 1996, pp. 45–46.

Even though Saddam was not a declared target of the air campaign, Coalition planners made a concerted effort to attack the facilities used by Saddam and other senior Iraqi officials. As GEN Norman Schwarzkopf, who commanded Coalition forces, put it: "At the very top of our target lists were the bunkers where we knew [Saddam] and his senior commanders were likely to be working."[16] Brent Scowcroft, President Bush's National Security Adviser, also agreed that a deliberate effort was made to eliminate Saddam.[17] Among the targets that were struck by Coalition aircraft were the facilities known or suspected to be personally used by Saddam, including the presidential residences and palace and the presidential and national command-and-control bunkers.

On July 12, 1993, U.S. Cobra gunships and ground forces attacked one of General Aideed's headquarters in Mogadishu during a meeting of senior SNA officials and Habr Gidr elders. The avowed objective of the attack was to "eliminate the SNA command center and its occupants" and to seize arms, documents, and communications equipment.[18] However, senior United Nations (UN) officials averred that Aideed himself was not a target, although this assertion is disputed by other well-placed sources.[19]

---

[16]In *It Doesn't Take a Hero*, New York: Linda Grey Bantam Books, 1992, pp. 318–319, H. Norman Schwarzkopf (GEN, USA, Ret.) writes that his and the other assertions by U.S. officials that the United States was not trying to kill Saddam were only "true, to a point." For other accounts of the purposes and conduct of Coalition air operations against leadership targets, see Rick Atkinson, *Crusade: The Untold Story of the Persian Gulf War*, New York: Houghton Mifflin Company, 1993, pp. 272–274, 473; Michael R. Gordon and Bernard B. Trainor (LtGen., USMC, Ret.), *The General's War: The Inside Story of the Conflict in the Gulf*, Boston: Little, Brown & Co., 1995, pp. 100, 137–138, 199, 313–314, 410–411; and U.S. Department of Defense, *Conduct of the Persian Gulf War: Final Report to Congress*, Washington, D.C.: U.S. Government Printing Office, April 1992, pp. 95–96, 150.

[17]In an ABC News interview, General Scowcroft did not disagree with the statement that the United States had "deliberately set out to kill" Saddam. Scowcroft stated, "We don't do assassinations, but yes we targeted all the places where Saddam might have been." When asked, "So you deliberately set out to kill him if you possibly could?" Scowcroft replied, "Yes, that's fair enough." See Peter Jennings, "Unfinished Business: The CIA and Saddam Hussein," report, ABC News, June 26, 1997.

[18]John L. Hirsch and Robert B. Oakley, *Somalia and Operation Restore Hope*, Washington, D.C.: United States Institute of Peace Press, 1995, p. 121, note 17.

[19]Donatella Lorch, "U.N. Says It Will Press Effort to Disarm Somalis," *New York Times*, July 14, 1993a, p. A6. However, John Drysdale, a senior UN adviser in Mogadishu,

Allied spokesmen also asserted that the April 22, 1999, NATO cruise missile attack on Slobodan Milosevic's official residence in Belgrade and the subsequent repeated attacks on the Dobanovci presidential villa and its associated command-and-control bunker were not aimed at assassinating the president of the Federal Republic of Yugoslavia (FRY).[20] While the republic's officials described the attack on the Belgrade residence as "an assassination attempt," Pentagon spokesman Kenneth Bacon disagreed, describing the residence as a legitimate military target that included "security and military bunkers" and functioned as a "command-and-control bunker." According to Bacon, NATO's aim was to attack "the head of the military regime" so as "to cut that off and break the central nervous system" of the FRY's military.[21]

SITUATIONS IN WHICH DIRECT ATTACKS ARE LIKELY TO BE SANCTIONED

The experience to date suggests that American decisionmakers may be willing to sanction direct military attacks that might kill enemy heads of state and other senior leaders so long as the attacks can be

- justified under the right of self-defense as protecting important U.S. national interests

- said to be directed against enemy facilities that serve a military or security function, such as command and control

- conducted by uniformed members of the armed services in accordance with the law of armed conflict (e.g., observing the rules of proportionality and necessity and avoiding, when possible, civilian casualties)

---

reports that Aideed was a target. See John Drysdale, *Whatever Happened in Somalia?* London: HAAN Associates, 1994, p. 203.

[20]General Wesley K. Clark, Supreme Allied Commander, Europe, reportedly helped identify a target associated with Milosevic's residence at Dobanovci where the FRY president "might have gone to ground." See Michael Ignatieff, "The Virtual Commander: How NATO Invented a New Kind of War," *New Yorker*, August 2, 1999, p. 30.

[21]See Michael Dobbs, "Allied Strike Denounced as 'Attempt on Milosevic,'" *Washington Post*, April 23, 1999, p. A33, and Bradley Graham, "Missiles Hit State TV, Residence of Milosevic," *Washington Post*, April 23, 1999, p. A33.

- embedded in a larger military campaign in which other targets are being attacked as well.

Finally, decisionmakers will also be more willing to sanction leadership attacks if they believe the targeted leader is the key or sole promoter and facilitator of the policy and behavior that the United States desires to change. There was every reason to believe, for example, that Iraq's invasion of and later attempt to hold onto Kuwait were primarily, if not exclusively, the result of Saddam Hussein's personal decisionmaking. Similarly, Qaddafi was clearly the prime mover behind Libya's export of terrorism and revolution during the mid-1980s. Similarly, Osama bin Laden has been the key organizer, leader, and financial backer of the Al-Qaeda terrorist network, which continues to attack U.S. civilian and military personnel both within the United States and around the world. Bin Laden is believed to have been responsible for the catastrophic loss of life that resulted from the September 11, 2001, hijackings and attacks on the New York's World Trade Center and on the Pentagon.

However, except in the case of a notorious terrorist, such as Osama bin Laden, decisionmakers will generally be loath to concede that specific enemy leaders are the targets of U.S. attack. They will be particularly reluctant to authorize attacks that might be perceived as clear-cut assassination attempts, such as the employment of ruses to lure foreign leaders to sites where they will be vulnerable to attack.[22]

These restraints will apply even in cases where it has been a longstanding U.S. policy to bring the leader down. When asked in February 1998 to comment on congressional suggestions that the United States should develop plans to kill Saddam Hussein, President Clinton said "it was against U.S. policy, based on an executive order put in place by President Ford, to design military plans aimed at killing other world leaders." It was Clinton's view that Executive Order 12333 mandates that "political killing or assassination, if you

---

[22]During the planning of the 1985 raid on Libya, a scheme was reportedly put forward at one of the Reagan administration's Crisis Pre-Planning Group meetings to lure Qaddafi to his compound on the night it was to be struck. The scheme was poorly thought out but was also rejected on the grounds that it would have been an "assassination plot," pure and simple. See David C. Martin and John Walcott, *Best Laid Plans: The Inside Story of America's War Against Terrorism*, New York: Harper & Row, 1988, p. 296.

will, is against [U.S.] foreign policy interests." "Would the Iraqi people be better off if there were a change in leadership?" Clinton asked. "I certainly think they would be. But that is not what the United Nations authorized us to do."[23]

ASSESSING THE RISKS AND BENEFITS OF DIRECT ATTACKS

As noted above, one of the key assumptions underlying attacks on leaders is the belief that the attacks will produce the coercive or deterrent effect desired. Most such attacks aim either to force a change in enemy policy by intimidating a leader to change his policy (if the attack misses) or to bring to power a successor who will adopt a different policy (if the attack succeeds). There may also be the assumption that even if the enemy's policy does not change, the elimination of a leader will weaken the enemy's war effort by causing a succession struggle or by bringing to power a leader with less charisma or competence.

Before ordering a leadership attack, decisionmakers must try to assess the potential risks and benefits of the attacks. Typically, such assessments will be hampered by gaps in the decisionmaker's information about the situation in the enemy camp and by his limited insight into the potential unintended consequences of the attack. One key question will be the probable orientation and competence of the leader who is likely to succeed to power in the event the incumbent were to be killed.

It is doubtful that many future risk/benefit assessments will be as uncomplicated as the one conducted by U.S. Admiral Chester Nimitz when he decided to intercept Admiral Isoroku Yamamoto's aircraft on its flight to Bougainville Island on April 18, 1943. Nimitz asked his intelligence officer: "Do we try to get him? If we did, could they replace him with someone better?" Upon receiving a negative reply,

---

[23]At the time of the confrontation with Iraq over UN inspections in February 1998, a number of U.S. lawmakers "called for a military plan aimed not just at coercing the Iraqis to allow unfettered United Nations weapons inspections, but at killing Saddam." See Mary Ann Akers, "Legality of Killing Saddam Debated," *Washington Times*, February 6, 1998, p. A12.

Nimitz said, "All right, we'll try it."[24] The elimination of Yamamoto was a net plus in that news of the widely respected admiral's demise depressed Japanese military and civilian morale. However, it is doubtful that Yamamoto's absence from the command structure appreciably harmed Japan's subsequent military conduct of the war.

As the following analysis will show, leadership attacks rarely produce positive outcomes even as modest as that of Yamamoto. An examination of past cases shows that direct attacks on leaders

- rarely produce wanted policy changes
- often fail to deter unwanted enemy behavior
- sometimes produce harmful unintended consequences
- frequently fail to kill the leader.

DIRECT ATTACKS RARELY PRODUCE WANTED POLICY CHANGES

Political Assassinations Typically Prove Ineffective

Experience shows that the demise of a targeted leader rarely produces the changes in government policy and practice anticipated. Historical analyses of the effects of political assassinations in both peacetime and war document the infrequency with which the killing of a particular leader has produced the results hoped for by the assassin. In addressing the question "Does assassination work?" one historian who examined the effects of assassinations from antiquity through modern times concluded

> The history of countless assassinations, examined with an eye to comparing apparent motives with actual outcomes, contains almost none that produced results consonant with the aims of the doer, assuming those aims to have extended at all beyond the miserable taking of a life.[25]

---

[24]Spector, Ronald H., *Eagle Against the Sun*, New York: The Free Press, 1985, pp. 227–228. For a discussion of the shootdown, see also Hiroyuki Agawa, *The Reluctant Admiral: Yamamoto and the Imperial Navy*, Tokyo: Kodansha International Ltd., 1979, pp. 369–379.

[25]Franklin L. Ford, *Political Murder: From Tyrannicide to Terrorism*, Cambridge, Mass.: Harvard University Press, 1985, p. 387.

Another analysis of the effects of the killing of important political personages during modern times found that

> the impact of an assassination on the political system tends to be low . . . . In most cases . . . success (from the point of view of the assassin) is at best incomplete. Either no change takes place at all or the changes that do occur are incongruent with those desired by the assassin. Indeed one can say more than this: on most occasions, assassinations result in utter failure as far as the political aims of the conspirators are concerned, especially if these conspirators expect to profit politically from the deed.[26]

Revolutionary Movements May Even Survive Loss of Their Founding Leaders

Some Movements Weakened Through the Capture and Apostasy of Their Leaders. Since the turn of the century, there have been several instances where the capture and subsequent apostasy of a particularly charismatic guerrilla leader have seriously weakened antigovernment rebellions. The capture of Philippine rebel leader Emilio Aquinaldo in 1901, for example, greatly reduced the armed resistance to the U.S. occupation of the Philippines. Once in American hands, Aquinaldo issued a proclamation calling on all insurgents to "lay down their arms and submit to American rule." This appeal prompted the surrender of five of Aquinaldo's seven regional commanders along with their troops.[27]

The Shining Path guerrilla movement in Peru was badly crippled by the 1992 capture in a Lima safe house of its founding father and leader, Abimael Guzman. Guzman's capture proved particularly demoralizing to his followers because he subsequently "deserted" to the government side while in jail, calling on his former comrades to

---

[26]Murray Clark Havens, Carl Leiden, and Karl M. Schmitt, *The Politics of Assassination*, Englewood Cliffs, N.J.: Prentice-Hall, Inc., 1970, pp. 148–149.

[27]See Uldarico S. Baclagon, *Philippine Campaigns*, Manila: Graphic House, 1952, p. 127; David Howard Bain, *Sitting in Darkness: Americans in the Philippines*, New York: Penguin Books, 1984, p. 385; and Bruce A. Ross (LCDR, USN), "The Case for Targeting Leadership in War," *Naval War College Review*, Winter 1993, p. 78.

give up their arms and form a political party.[28] The Shining Path movement became fractionalized after Guzman's incarceration and has since been progressively weakened by the subsequent capture of other leaders, which has caused many of the guerrillas to lay down their arms.[29]

A similar pattern seems to have followed the 1998 capture and subsequent jail-cell political conversion of Kurdish rebel leader Abdullah Ocalan. During his trial in a Turkish court, Ocalan called on the Kurdish Workers' Party (PKK) fighters he commanded to give up their armed struggle.[30] After Ocalan was sentenced to death on treason charges in June 1999, subordinate PKK leaders—no doubt partly motivated by the desire to save their leader from hanging—"pledged to abide by Ocalan's order to end their insurgency, to withdraw from Turkish territory and to transform themselves into a peaceful political movement."[31] Although gravely weakened, the PKK remains a residual presence in parts of southeastern Turkey.[32]

However, the removal of the architect of an enemy's war policy does not always result in its weakening. This is particularly true when the belligerent state or insurgent organization is governed by a collective leadership or has second-echelon leaders who are strongly motivated to continue a struggle.

The Death of Ho Chi Minh. Ho's death from natural causes in September 1969 during the midst of the Vietnam War did not in any measurable way impede North Vietnam's war effort or deflect the Hanoi regime from its goal of "liberating the South." The line of succession within the Hanoi leadership was firmly established within

---

[28]See Calvin Sims, "On the Trail of Peru's Maoist Rebels," *New York Times*, August 8, 1996, p. A12.

[29]The principal leader who tried to reorganize the movement after Guzman's arrest, Oscar Ramirez Durand, Shining Path's military strategist, was captured in 1999. See Anthony Faiola, "Shining Path's Leading Light Is Captured Without a Fight," *Guardian Weekly*, July 22–28, 1999, p. 32.

[30]Ocalan described the uprising as "a mistake" and renounced any demands for Kurdish independence or even autonomy. See Selcan Hacaoglu, "PKK Leader Pleads for His Life," *Washington Times*, June 1, 1999, p. A9, and Amberin Zaman, "Kurds' Surrender Awakens Turkish Doves," *Washington Post*, October 7, 1999, p. 27.

[31]Zaman (1999), p. 27.

[32]See U.S. Department of State, *Turkey—Consular Information Sheet*, October 2, 2000c.

the North Vietnamese Politburo, as was the Politburo's war policy. As one U.S. general officer put it, after Ho's death "the Hanoi regime continued its unrelenting and uncompromising outlook without a change of beat."[33] Vietnamese communist cadres of all levels continued to use Ho's name and words to extract even greater sacrifices from the military and civilian populations under their control.

Russian Attacks on Chechen Leaders. During the course of the war in Chechnya, the Russian military and secret service made repeated attempts to capture or eliminate the leaders of the Chechen separatist movement.   On April 21, 1996, the Chechen president, Dzhokhar Dudayev, was killed by a Russian missile while making a telephone call from a portable satellite dish in a copse near a village 20 miles southwest of Grozny. It is believed that the missile was air launched and guided to home in on Dudayev's satellite signal. This was the last of a series of Russian attempts to eliminate Dudayev, who had found it necessary to change locations constantly to elude the Russian secret services.[34]

In an interview shortly before his death, Dudayev reported that he had "lost count" of the number of assassination attempts made on him since 1991. The Russian secret services had "done everything to catch him," including "planting bugs in his car and giving one of his bodyguards at the peace talks a present of a commando knife with a transmitter concealed in the handle so that bomber planes could hunt him down."[35]

While Dudayev's removal from the scene may have given Boris Yeltsin a temporary political boost by clearing the way for peace negotiations with the Chechen separatists prior to the July 9, 1996, Russian presidential elections, his death did little if anything to further Russian objectives in Chechnya. The Chechen commanders and fighters were "determined to be seen to abide by their constitution and united in their desire not to let Russia exploit any internal differences," and accepted the succession to power of Dudayev's vice

---

[33]GEN Bruce Palmer, Jr., *The 25-Year War: America's Military Role in Vietnam*, Lexington, Ky.: The University Press of Kentucky, 1984, p. 119.

[34]Carlotta Gall and Thomas de Waal, : *Calamity in the Caucasus*, New York: New York University Press, 1998, pp. 318–323.

[35]Gall and de Waal (1998), p. 323.

president, Zelimkhan Yandarbiyev.[36] They also remained steadfast in their commitment to wrest independence for Chechnya.

Less than a week after Yeltsin's reelection, the Russians mounted another coup de main, this time aimed at eliminating the remaining Chechen rebel leadership. In a calculated act and without provocation, the Russians broke the peace agreement they had recently negotiated with the Chechens by bombing the mountain village where virtually the entire Chechen leadership had gathered for a meeting. The bombing was followed by an airborne assault by Russian paratroopers to cut off escape routes from the village.

The operation proved to be a failure, as all the Chechen leaders got out safely. In response to this perfidy, the Chechen commanders resolved to go on the offensive and retake the Chechen capital of Grozny.[37] The recapture of Grozny by Chechen rebel infiltrators in August 1996 led to a new peace agreement, this time negotiated by Yeltsin's special envoy, General Alexander Lebed, that called for a total Russian military withdrawal from Chechnya.[38]

Following the August 1999 attack in Dagestan by a Chechen separatist group and the September 1999 bombings of two Moscow apartment buildings, Russian troops reentered Chechnya in October 1999 for the purported purpose of eliminating "foreign terrorists" from the North Caucasus.[39] By spring 2000, Russian forces controlled most Chechen territory, but the conflict continued as resistance fighters regularly ambushed federal convoys and troops.[40] Indeed, from all appearances, the Chechen resistance continues to

---

[36]Yandarbiyev remained Chechen president until losing the presidential election in January 1997. Gall and de Waal (1998), pp. 324, 378.

[37]Gall and de Waal (1998), pp. 329–330.

[38]Gall and de Waal (1998), pp. 357–361.

[39]Russian authorities accused the Chechen government leaders of failing to halt rebel activities and failing to curb hostage taking and banditry in the republic. Russian officials also alleged that the Moscow bombings and similar explosions in other areas of the Russian Federation were the work of insurgent groups from Chechnya and Dagestan. However, they presented no evidence linking Chechen separatists to the bombings. See U.S. Department of State, *Patterns of Global Terrorism: 1999*, Washington, D.C.: April 2000a, and U.S. Department of State, *Background Notes: Russia*, May 2000b.

[40]U.S. Department of State (2000b).

be led by individuals no less committed than was Dudayev to their country's independence from Moscow.

DIRECT ATTACKS OFTEN FAIL TO DETER UNWANTED ENEMY BEHAVIOR

The deterrent effect of leadership attacks also has yet to be proven. It is difficult to find instances where punitive attacks against enemy leaders or terrorists have reformed their behavior. The concerted Coalition attempts to eliminate Saddam Hussein during the Gulf War and its aftermath have not deterred the Iraqi leader from organizing an assassination attempt against former President Bush, repressing the marsh Arabs, invading the Kurd areas of northern Iraq, defying UN Security Council resolutions, ousting UN WMD inspectors, or attempting to militarily contest the allied no-fly zones. Obviously, the U.S. attempt on Osama bin Laden's life did not dissuade the terrorist leader from ordering further attacks on the U.S. homeland, embassies, and armed forces.

Those who see a deterrent value in leadership attack often point to the Israeli retaliations against terrorists and the U.S. bombing of Qaddafi as evidence of the efficacy of punitive responses. However, an examination of the record with regard to these cases provides little support for this thesis.

Israel's Countermeasures Against Terrorism

It has long been Israel's policy to respond forcefully to terrorist attacks and threats against its citizens. Israeli countermeasures have aimed both to reduce the terrorist capabilities and propensities to strike and to limit the damage terrorist attacks can inflict.[41] In addition to a wide range of passive defense measures, Israeli countermeasures have focused on (1) counterforce operations designed to reduce terrorist resources, (2) impeding operations designed to intercept terrorist strikes, and (3) punishment operations mounted in response to completed strikes.[42]

---

[41]Hanan Alon, *Countering Palestinian Terrorism in Israel: Toward a Policy Analysis of Countermeasures*, Santa Monica, Calif.: RAND, N-1567-FF, 1980, p. 69.

[42]Alon (1980), pp. 68–69.

Israel's counterforce, impeding, and punishment operations have been targeted at both terrorist leaders and rank and file. Over the years, numerous air, naval, and ground force strikes have been mounted against suspected terrorists and terrorist sites outside Israel, and a variety of clandestine attacks have been conducted against individual terrorists by a unit of Israel's Central Institute for Intelligence and Special Missions (Mossad). While these operations have no doubt impeded and even prevented terrorist strikes in some cases, countermeasures aimed at individual terrorists seem to have had marginal deterrent value.

An analysis of Israeli strikes against Palestinian terrorism from 1967 to 1978 produced by an Israel Defense Force officer conversant with Israeli countermeasures found "no proof that the strikes reduced the willingness of Palestinians to join the organizations and die for their cause." The study's author went on to write: "one may assume that, on the contrary, the strikes led to rage which may have encouraged joining terror organizations and taking part in their operations."[43]

Another assessment, written in 1998, concluded that Israel had experienced little success in its attempt "to frighten and deter terrorists and disrupt their plans for future violence."[44] Even though Mossad's clandestine unit had reportedly eliminated more than a dozen "master terrorists" over the years, it was asserted that this had not ended the threat. "Those who were assassinated were soon replaced and terrorism resumed, sometimes more ferociously than before." The assessment went on to assert that

> except for Mr. [Ariel] Sharon and Prime Minister Netanyahu himself, most Cabinet ministers and many senior Mossad officials publicly and privately acknowledge the ineffectiveness of assassination as a weapon in the war against terrorism.[45]

---

[43]Alon (1980), pp. 80–81.

[44]Yossi Melman, "Israel's Darkest Secrets," *New York Times*, March 25, 1998, p. A27.

[45]Melman (1998), p. A27. Some Israeli intelligence officials argue that the elimination of leaders of "small terrorist groups" has proven effective, in that it has disrupted the groups and compelled their successor leaders to "spend considerable energy keeping low." Even if retaliation does not deter further terrorist attacks, some observers see the Israeli attacks on terrorist leaders as helping to buttress public morale. As Ehud Sprinzak, a professor at Hebrew University, put it: "When you consider that terrorism

Some of the Mossad operations directed at specific targets provoked damaging retaliation or proved counterproductive in other respects. In the view of at least some "wise and experienced Israeli intelligence officials," the 1996 "successful" assassination of a Palestinian terrorist leader in Gaza led directly to a series of retaliatory suicide bombings that cost a number of Israeli lives.[46] A different example of counterproductive effects was provided by Mossad's 1997 botched assassination attempt against a subordinate Hamas leader in Amman, Jordan. The attempted killing strained Israeli-Jordanian relations and forced the Israelis to release the senior Hamas spiritual leader they had previously held in captivity.[47]

During the intifada that began in late 2000, Israeli forces adopted a "tactic of hunting down and killing individual Palestinian militants whom Israel [held] responsible for planning attacks on or attacking its citizens."[48] In a break with their past reticence to openly discuss assassination operations, senior Israeli officials publicly acknowledged this new "liquidations" policy. While Israeli officials asserted that the tactic was effective in thwarting attacks and degrading the Palestinians' operational capability, Palestinian officials claimed the attacks were counterproductive and simply added "fuel to the fire" on the Palestinian streets.[49] Given the escalating violence witnessed

---

is largely a psychological weapon, psychology is very important in the fight against terror. Sometimes you have to boost the morale of your own people." Still others see Israel as having little choice but to employ assassination. Yossi Melman, a writer on security matters for the newspaper *Ha'aretz*, summed up the problem facing Israel as follows: "What else do you do? You're involved in a game where you do not set the rules. There's no other way for the state to protect itself except through a balance of terror, through revenge." See Serge Schmemann, "Hit Parade: The Harsh Logic of Assassination," *New York Times*, Week in Review, October 12, 1997, pp. 1, 4.

[46]Raymond Close, "Hard Targets: We Can't Defeat Terrorism with Bombs and Bombast," *Washington Post*, August 30, 1998, pp. C1, C5.

[47]See the *Washington Times* interview with Geoffrey Kemp, "Botched Assassination Boosts Hamas, Hurts Netanyahu-Hussein Bond," October 8, 1997, and Paul Koring, "Mossad Again Finds Itself in Public Glare: Amman Fiasco Recalls '73 Incident," *Washington Times*, October 8, 1997, p. A14. See also Youssef M. Ibrahim, "Jordan Is Angered by Israeli Findings on Assassination Fiasco," *New York Times*, February 18, 1998, p. A7.

[48]See Deborah Sontag, "Israel Acknowledges Hunting Down Arab Militants," *New York Times*, December 22, 2000, p. A10.

[49]Among other effects, the Israelis claimed that the assassinations had a "chilling effect on Palestinian paramilitary operations," forced well-known Palestinian commanders to keep a "lower profile," and "undermined the confidence of Palestinian

in the area during 2001, it is difficult to demonstrate that the new Israeli "liquidation" policy had either significantly stemmed Palestinian street violence or reduced suicide bombings and other attacks against Israeli citizens.

The 1986 U.S. Raid Against Libya

One of the objectives of the 1986 Operation El Dorado Canyon air strikes on Libya was to dissuade Qaddafi from engaging in further terrorist attacks on Americans and U.S. allies. In his television address to the nation announcing the raids, President Reagan expressed the hope that the air strikes would both "diminish Colonel Qaddafi's capacity to export terror" and "provide him with incentives and reasons to alter his criminal behavior." The president warned, "Tonight we have done what we had to do. If necessary, we shall do it again."[50] In a private communication to Prime Minister Margaret Thatcher requesting the use of British bases for the raid, the president assessed the likely effect of the attacks as follows:

> I have no illusion that these actions will eliminate the terrorist threat. But it will show that officially sponsored terrorist actions by a government—such as Libya has repeatedly perpetuated—will not be without cost. The loss of such state sponsorship will inevitably weaken the ability of terrorist organizations to carry out their criminal attacks even as we work through diplomatic, political, and economic channels to alleviate the more fundamental causes of such terrorism.[51]

Even though the U.S. attack on Qaddafi's residence in the Azziziyah Barracks compound missed hitting Qaddafi directly, it reportedly left the Libyan leader psychologically shaken. Laser-guided bombs detonated within 50 feet of Qaddafi's headquarters-residence and caused considerable damage to the compound. The bombing

---

militiamen." See Sontag (2000); see also Deborah Sontag, "Israel Hunts Down and Kills a Top Arafat Security Officer," *New York Times*, February 14, 2001, p. A3; and Matt Rees, "The Work of Assassins," *Time*, January 15, 2001, pp. 36–39.

[50]Quoted in Joseph T. Stanik, *"Swift and Effective Retribution": The U.S. Sixth Fleet and the Confrontation with Qaddafi, The U.S. Navy in the Modern World Series*, No. 3, Washington, D.C.: Naval Historical Center, Department of the Navy, 1996, p. 49.

[51]Margaret Thatcher, *The Downing Street Years*, New York: HarperCollins, 1993, p. 444.

reportedly killed Qaddafi's adopted 15-month-old daughter and seriously injured two of his sons.[52] Some accounts also list Qaddafi's wife among the injured.[53] Qaddafi escaped unharmed, apparently because he was in his underground bunker at the time of the attack.[54]

The attack, however, had its effects. In the months immediately following the El Dorado attack, Qaddafi reportedly suffered bouts of severe paranoia, apparently because of fears of another air attack or an American-backed assassination:

> He abandoned his headquarters at [Azziziyah Barracks], and moved around the country in an armored bus. He faltered and his mind seemed to wander in the few taped speeches he made, though staff members said this was due largely to the strain of never sleeping in the same place two nights in a row.[55]

Eyewitnesses described Qaddafi as "shaken, confused, and uncharacteristically subdued."[56]

Immediately following the raid, there was a dramatic rise in terrorist events targeting Americans and American property abroad. One analysis counted 18 such events in April 1986.[57] Some of these terrorist events may have been sparked by provocative Libyan

---

[52]Stanik (1996), pp. 41, 45.

[53]Edward Schumacher, "The United States and Libya," *Foreign Affairs*, Winter 1986/1987, p. 335, and Stanik (1996), p. 45.

[54]Vice Admiral Frank Kelso, Commander, U.S. Sixth Fleet, stated after the attack that the U.S. aircraft did not carry "ordnance to go after deep bunkers." The absence of such weapons and Qaddafi's well-known propensity to change locations frequently make it unlikely that U.S. planners had high confidence that the attack would kill the Libyan dictator. However, there can be little doubt that U.S. officials hoped Qaddafi would be one of the casualties of the air strikes and had consciously structured the raid "in a way that made Qaddafi's death possible." See Brian L. Davis, *Qaddafi, Terrorism, and the Origins of the U.S. Attack on Libya*, New York: Praeger, 1990, p. 122, and Tim Zimmermann, "Coercive Diplomacy and Libya," in Alexander L. George & William E. Simons, eds., *The Limits of Coercive Diplomacy*, Second Edition, Boulder, Colo.: Westview Press, 1994, p. 204.

[55]Schumacher (1986/1987), p. 336.

[56]Stanik (1996), p. 49.

[57]Henry W. Prunckun, Jr., *Operation El Dorado Canyon: A Military Solution to the Law Enforcement Problem of Terrorism: A Quantitative Analysis*, dissertation, University of South Australia, Wayville, South Australia: Slezak Associates, 1994, p. 48.

broadcast messages calling on Arab listeners to attack American persons and facilities.[58] Other events are believed to have been more directly the result of Libyan action, including the killing of one of the American and three of the British hostages then held in Lebanon, the shooting of an American embassy official in the Sudan and another in South Yemen, and the foiled terrorist operation to attack the U.S. Air Force officers' club in Turkey.[59]

In July 1986, nine Libyan-sponsored terrorists were arrested in Togo for planning to bomb a marketplace and the U.S. embassy in Benin. In August, terrorists whom the British believed were under Libyan control, attacked the United Kingdom base at Akrotiri on Cyprus and a crowded beach near the base.[60]

The El Dorado Canyon raid, however, also apparently led Qaddafi to eventually reduce the visibility and incidence of Libya's involvement in terrorist activities. While not disavowing terrorism as an instrument of state policy, Qaddafi did mute his rhetoric in support of terrorist groups.[61] After the spate of reprisal attacks against American and British targets in the immediate aftermath of the raid, the number of terrorist incidents linked to Libya began to decline.

As reported by the U.S. State Department, the number of terrorist incidents involving Libya "dropped from 19 in 1986 to 6 each in 1987 and 1988."[62] A quantitative analysis of all terrorist events through November 1987 also noted a worldwide drop-off in "high-severity" and "medium-severity" terrorist events in the months following the initial surge of reprisal attacks. However, the number of "low-severity" events increased significantly during the same period.[63]

Some of this reduction in Libyan terrorist activity may have resulted from the cutbacks and restrictions imposed on Libya's diplomatic

---

[58]Prunckun (1994), p. 48, note 38.

[59]The Libyans also made an abortive attempt to strike back by launching two missiles at the U.S. Coast Guard station located on the Italian island of Lampedusa. See Martin and Walcott (1988), pp. 313–314, and Stanik (1996), pp. 48–49.

[60]Zimmermann (1994), p. 217.

[61]Stanik (1996), p. 49.

[62]Stanik (1996), p. 49.

[63]Prunckun (1994), pp. 49–53.

officials in Europe, which degraded Qaddafi's capabilities to mount terrorist operations. Apparently galvanized by the prospect of U.S. military action against Libya, the members of the European Economic Community imposed their first meaningful sanctions against Libya on the eve of the April 15 raid by "reducing the number of Libyan diplomats in their countries and tightening surveillance on those remaining." Additional sanctions were enacted following the raid, including restrictions of the movements of Libyan diplomats, agreements not to admit Libyans suspected of involvement in terrorism, and further cutbacks in the size of Libya's "People's Bureau" diplomatic missions and student presence in particular European countries.[64] Qaddafi seems to have adopted a more disciplined approach to terrorist operations following the raid, enlisting more competent surrogates and striving to mask his personal involvement in particular terrorist operations.[65]

However, Qaddafi continued to employ terrorism against his perceived enemies. In December 1988, most likely as a delayed payback for the El Dorado Canyon raid, Qaddafi apparently arranged the sabotage of Pan Am Flight 103, which blew up over Lockerbie, Scotland, killing 270 persons, some 189 of whom were Americans. Less than a year later, in September 1989, Qaddafi apparently also repaid France for successfully opposing Libya's attempts to dominate Chad by having his agents plant a bomb on the French airliner UTA 772, which blew up over Niger in central Africa, killing 171 passengers and crew.[66]

---

[64]Martin and Walcott (1988), p. 314. Secretary of State George Shultz attributed the European crackdown on Libya to the fact that the Europeans were "more alert now to the dangers posed to them by Libya, alarmed at the use of force by the United States, and anxious to show cooperation with a popular U.S. action." Shultz (1993), p. 687.

[65]The U.S. State Department reported in 1988 "that it had 'seen no evidence that Libya has abandoned support of international terrorism, subversion, and aggression.'" See Stanik (1996), p. 49.

[66]Stanik (1996), p. 49. On January 31, 2001, a Scottish court found a Libyan intelligence official, Abdelbaset Ali Mohmed Al Megrahi, guilty of murder in the bombing of Pan Am Flight 103. A second defendant, Al Amin Khalifa Fhimah, indicted for the bombing, was set free because of a lack of evidence. In rendering their verdict on the Pan Am bombing, the Scottish judges concluded: "The clear inference which we draw from this evidence is that the conception, planning and execution of the plot which led to the planting of the explosive device was of Libyan origin." French officials concluded that the Libyan intelligence service was also responsible for the bombing of UTA 772 and named Qaddafi's brother-in-law, Muhammad al-Sanusi, as the master-

It is important to note that in the downing of Pan Am 103, Qaddafi killed far more Americans than were killed in the 1986 Berlin disco bombing that triggered El Dorado Canyon or in all other Libyan terrorist operations involving U.S. citizens. Yet, when U.S. leaders finally determined the Libyan source of the Pan Am bombing, they did not mount another military raid on Libya as previous U.S. leaders had threatened but instead opted to take the matter to the UN Security Council, which eventually imposed air travel and other commercial sanctions on Libya.[67] Although Libya has not been implicated in any international terrorist act for several years, the U.S. Secretary of State continues to count the Libyan government among its list of state sponsors of terrorism.[68]

DIRECT ATTACKS CAN SOMETIMES PRODUCE HARMFUL UNINTENDED CONSEQUENCES

The possibility that a leadership attack may not produce the desired changes in enemy policy and behavior may be a risk that at least some decisionmakers will be prepared to accept. What will be far less palatable to the decisionmaker will be unanticipated outcomes that prove contrary to the initiator's interests. As the Israeli experience and the cases discussed below suggest, leadership attacks can produce counterproductive and even catastrophic results.

---

mind of the attack. Given Qaddafi's tight control over his intelligence service, it is inconceivable that these terrorist operations could have occurred without his knowledge and direction. See Donald G. McNeil, Jr., "Libyan Convicted By Scottish Court in '88 Pan Am Blast," *New York Times*, January 1, 2001, pp. A1, A8, and Gerald Seenan, "How the Trap Closed on the Libyan Bomber," *Guardian Weekly*, February 8–14, 2001, p. 25.

[67]When Qaddafi initially refused to surrender the two suspects in the Pan Am bombing for trial, the United Nations banned international flights and the sale of certain aviation, oil, and defense equipment to Libya. While these and even more severe unilateral U.S. sanctions discouraged investment, made transport difficult, and increased import costs for Libya, they did not cripple the economy or significantly affect Libya's main industry and source of income, oil. See "Libya, Mystery of the Vanishing Oil Money," *Economist*, February 7, 1998, p. 48. However, the UN sanctions were sufficiently onerous that to get them suspended, Libya agreed to turn the suspects over to trial in the Netherlands. (See note 66, above.) The United States, however, continued to impose sanctions even after the January 31, 2001, verdict by the Scottish court, holding that Libya should accept responsibility for the bombing and pay compensation to the families of the victims. See Jane Perlez, "Unpersuaded by Verdict, Bush Backs Sanctions," *New York Times*, February 1, 2001, p. A8.

[68]U.S. Department of State (2000a).

The British Plans to Assassinate Hitler

The dilemmas and uncertainties decisionmakers sometimes face when contemplating possible unintended consequences are manifest in the debate that surrounded the British plot to assassinate Adolf Hitler.

In June 1944, the British Special Operations Executive (SOE) began to develop plans to kill Hitler. A number of schemes for assassinating the German leader were devised using such instruments as poisons, sniper attacks conducted by commandos in fake Nazi uniforms, and explosives placed underneath Hitler's personal train. All the designs were predicated on attacking the German leader either at his alpine residence at the Berghof above Berchtesgaden or on the train that carried him to or from the Berghof retreat. The schemes were given the code name Operation Foxley.[69]

Senior British officials both within and outside the SOE had sharply divided views about the desirability of killing Hitler. The proponents of assassination held that the German war effort would collapse almost immediately if Hitler were eliminated.[70] They argued that Hitler's death would break the "mystical hold" he had on the German population and bring the war to a rapid conclusion. As a senior SOE officer put it: "Remove Hitler, and there is nothing left."[71]

Those opposing assassination held that Hitler's removal would not accelerate war termination. They further argued that Hitler's "strategic blundering made him more of an asset to the Allies alive than dead" and that his elimination by enemy hands would ensure his martyrdom among the German population. In particular, opponents feared that a successful assassination would create a new "stab-in-the-back legend" and help promote the myth that Germany's forces had not been defeated militarily—perceptions similar to those that had poisoned politics in the Weimar Republic

---

[69]For a discussion of the operation, see Public Records Office, *Operation Foxley: The British Plan to Kill Hitler*, Kew, U.K., 1998. See also T. R. Reid, "British Spies Planned Many Deaths for Hitler," *Washington Post*, July 24, 1998a, p. A32, and, "Blow the Fuhrer from the Train and Other British Plots," *New York Times*, August 2, 1998, p. WK7.

[70]Public Records Office (1998), p. vii.

[71]Air Vice Marshal A. P. Ritchie, quoted in Warren Hoge, "Britain Reveals Elaborate Plots to Kill Hitler as War Neared End," *New York Times*, July 24, 1998, p. A10.

and facilitated the resurrection of German militarism after World War I.[72] Prime Minister Winston Churchill, among others, was convinced that the "elimination of Hitler would not be advantageous" and might prove "positively counterproductive."[73]

Writing in October 1944, a SOE officer argued that assassination would prove counterproductive over both the short and the longer terms:

> As a strategist, Hitler has been of the greatest possible assistance to the British war effort. To remove him from the wheel at a time when he and his fanatics have pledged themselves to defend every street and every house on German soil would almost inevitably canonize him and give birth to the myth that Germany would have been saved if he had lived.[74]

These arguments have carried over to the present day as historians still hold differing views about whether the elimination of Hitler by British hands after mid-1944, on balance, would have produced a positive or negative result.[75] Similar arguments have been raised about a successful German assassination of Hitler. One historian who speculated about the possible consequences that might have flowed had the July 20, 1944, German assassination attempt proved successful concluded that

> It would be placing an extraordinary high value on a single outcome—the peaceful internal development of postwar Germany—to suggest that such a result was worth the price of [the] last nine months of Hitler's war.[76]

As things turned out, none of the assassination schemes was ever acted upon. By the time the SOE's assassination plan was fully developed in spring 1945, the war was virtually over—and had it been attempted, it certainly would have failed. The plan contemplated at that point in time suffered from a fatal operational flaw:

---

[72]Public Records Office (1998), pp. vii–ix, and Hoge (1998), p. A10.

[73]Public Records Office (1998), p. 30.

[74]Quoted in "Blow the Fuhrer from the Train and Other British Plots" (1998), p. WK7.

[75]For a discussion of the possible desirable and undesirable consequences of a successful British assassination, see Public Records Office (1998), pp. vii–x.

[76]See Ford (1985), pp. 283–286.

Hitler was not at the Berghof. Allied intelligence was unable to keep track of Hitler's whereabouts, and as a consequence, the SOE's planning for an attack at the Berghof continued in "blissful ignorance" of the fact that Hitler had left Berchtesgaden nine months earlier, on July 14, 1944, "never to return."[77]

The Proposal to Bomb Hirohito's Palace

In a November 1944 memorandum to Henry (Hap) Arnold, Commander, U.S. Army Air Force, Lauris Norstad, Commander, the 20th Air Force, proposed that the Army Air Force commemorate the anniversary of Pearl Harbor by mounting a huge strike against Emperor Hirohito's palace in Tokyo. General Norstad indicated that "he had discussed the idea with experts in Japanese psychology, who felt that even a partial destruction of the palace would 'directly attack the Emperor's position of the invulnerable deity.'"[78] General Arnold did not act on the proposal, considering the idea premature.[79]

When weighing the potential downside of bombing the palace, General Norstad focused on the risk that the Japanese might mistreat and perhaps kill U.S. prisoners of war in retaliation.[80] What General Norstad could not foresee was the crucial role Hirohito was to play in facilitating Japan's surrender some nine months later. When the last wartime Japanese cabinet was split over accepting allied surrender terms in August 1944, it was the emperor who broke the deadlock by ordering the cabinet ministers to accept the Allied conditions. Hirohito's intervention and public declarations were also crucial to inducing many potentially obstructionist Japanese military officers to accept the decision to terminate the war.[81] Had Hirohito been killed in an air attack on the palace, the Pacific war would likely have

---

[77]Public Records Office (1998), pp. x, 30.

[78]Ronald Schaffer, *Wings of Judgment: American Bombing in World War II*, New York: Oxford University Press, 1985, p. 123.

[79]General Arnold wrote on Norstad's memo: "Not at this time. Our position—bombing factories, docks, etc. is sound. Later destroy whole city." Quoted in Schaffer (1985), p. 123.

[80]Schaffer (1985), p. 123.

[81]Robert J. C. Butow, *Japan's Decision to Surrender*, Stanford, Calif.: Stanford University Press, 1954, pp. 166–233.

continued longer, as Hirohito's successor, the 11-year-old Crown Prince Akihito, would have lacked the personal authority to influence such deliberations.

The Hijacking of Ben Bella in Algeria

From early on in the Algerian war, the French secret intelligence service had identified Ahmed Ben Bella as the "Number One leader" of the Front de Libération Nationale (FLN) revolt and had mounted abortive attempts to assassinate him.[82] In October 1956, French military personnel managed to capture Ben Bella and several of his colleagues by illegally ordering Ben Bella's Moroccan-owned but French-piloted aircraft to land on French-held Algerian territory. Ben Bella and his party had been en route to Tunis to attend a summit conference with the Tunisian and Moroccan heads of state to discuss the future conduct of the war and the furtherance of the peace initiatives that were then secretly under way with representatives of the French government.[83]

Contrary to the French military's view that the neutralization of Ben Bella would constitute a major blow to the FLN, his capture, in retrospect, turned out to be a major blunder, as it increased the militancy of both the FLN and its outside supporters. The Tunisian and Moroccan leaders, who prior to that point had been pressing the FLN toward a negotiated peace with France, were so affronted by the hijacking that they "henceforth stiffened their resolve to back the Algerian war effort to the utmost."[84]

More significantly, the capture of Ben Bella eliminated a widening rift and power struggle within the FLN command between the "exterior" leadership headed by Ben Bella, which concentrated on mobilizing international materiel and political support for the revolution, and the more hard-line "interior" FLN leaders, who directed most of the fighting. Secretly, the "interior" leaders were delighted by Ben Bella's capture and incarceration:

---

[82]Alistair Horne, *A Savage War of Peace: Algeria 1954–1962*, New York: Viking Press, 1977, p. 129.

[83]Horne (1977), pp. 159–160.

[84]Horne (1977), p. 160.

[U]nity had been restored and all argument about the primacy of the "interior" resolved—because now the "exterior" had simply ceased to exist. Any flagging by potential "soft-liners" had been effectively quelled. Thus had the French army devisors of the coup really done the enemy a good turn. Whatever else, the Ben Bella episode undoubtedly marked a major turning-point in the war. From now on the war could only proceed savagely and irreconcilably; any other way out had been sealed off.[85]

Ben Bella and his captured colleagues remained in French custody for four and one-half years. As a result of their prolonged incarceration, they grew increasingly embittered and intransigent and became "a source of constant embarrassment to successive French governments, a veritable time-bomb in their midst." Ben Bella and the other prisoners eventually became so unforgiving and implacably militant toward the French that they were among the "hardest of the hard-liners" when setting terms for ending the war. During the subsequent peace talks with the French, Ben Bella strove to persuade FLN negotiators to oppose "any dilution of future Algerian sovereignty, or the continuance of French influence in Algeria in any form whatsoever." French interest suffered a further blow when Ben Bella became the first president of Algeria in 1962.[86]

The 1993 U.S. Attacks on SNA Positions in Mogadishu

Leadership attacks aimed at producing beneficial results can prove counterproductive when the assumptions underlying the operations fail to reflect existing cultural, political, and military realities. Such was the case in Mogadishu, Somalia, during June and July of 1993, when, following an SNA ambush of Pakistani peacekeepers, U.S. and other UN Operation in Somalia (UNOSOM) II forces mounted air and ground attacks on weapon caches, radio facilities, and headquarters sites belonging to General Mohamed Farah Aideed and the SNA.[87] While these attacks were militarily effective in reducing the

---

[85]Horne (1977), p. 161.

[86]Horne (1977), pp. 468–469.

[87]Twenty-four Pakistanis were killed and scores of others injured. In response to this attack, the UN Security Council on June 6, 1993, adopted Resolution 837, which reemphasized the need for the early disarmament of all Somali parties and the neutraliza-

SNA's immediate weapon inventories and neutralizing Aideed's radio, their political and psychological effects were counterproductive. Designed to destroy Aideed's power base, the attacks instead resulted in increased Somali support for Aideed and intensified Somali opposition to U.S. and UN forces.

From the standpoint of Somali perceptions, the most important of these attacks occurred on July 12, 1993, when U.S. Cobra gunships and ground forces assaulted one of Aideed's headquarters in Mogadishu during a meeting of senior SNA officials and Habr Gidr elders.[88] The attack aimed to "cripple" the SNA's command structure and, if possible, Aideed himself, as well as to capture arms, documents, and communications equipment.[89] The strike, which had been "approved in advance up the entire U.S. chain of command to the White House," was conducted without warning.[90] It was the first time U.S. or UN forces in Somalia had targeted people instead of buildings and arms depots.[91] The Cobras fired some 16 missiles into the building in "an attempt to eliminate the SNA command center and its occupants."[92]

---

tion of radio broadcasting systems that contributed to the violence and attacks directed against UNOSOM II. Without naming Aideed specifically, the resolution essentially called for Aideed's arrest, trial, and punishment. See UN Security Council Resolution 837 (1993).

[88] According to John Drysdale, the purpose of the Somali meeting was to explain the findings of a meeting held on the previous day "concerning a renewal of dialogue between the SNA and UNOSOM II." See Drysdale (1994), pp. 202–203.

[89] The target of the attack was a house owned by Aideed's defense minister, Abdi Qaybdiid. See Keith B. Richburg, "In War on Aideed, UN Battled Itself: Internal Conflict Stymied Decisions of Military Operations," *Washington Post*, December 6, 1993,.

[90] Hirsch and Oakley (1995), p. 121. According to Elizabeth Drew, President Clinton personally approved the gunship attack. She quotes Anthony Lake, then President Clinton's National Security Adviser, as saying that they had approved the attack, "But nobody was supposed to be killed." See Georgie Anne Geyer, "Syndrome That Began in Somalia," *Washington Times*, October 3, 1998, p. 19.

[91] According to Keith Richburg, "The Cobra gunners had a specific purpose—to kill everyone inside. They accomplished their mission with deadly accuracy, first blasting away the stairwells to prevent escape, then pounding missiles into the top floors of the old, whitewashed villa." Apparently, this mode of attack was chosen both because U.S. officials wanted to hold down U.S. casualties when "trying to catch Aideed" and because Pakistani troops had "refused to surround the house so that those meeting inside could be forced out and arrested." See Richburg (1993).

[92] Hirsch and Oakley (1995), p. 121.

The number killed in the attack remains a matter of dispute. American officials claimed that no more than 20 died and that all of those were "top Aideed militia leaders," whereas the Somalis claimed some 73 were killed, including religious leaders and elders of the Habr Gidr subclan.[93] As previously mentioned, there is also some dispute as to whether Aideed was a target of the attack. American officials asserted that he was not a target, as he rarely attended such meetings.[94] However, John Drysdale suggests that Aideed was a target in that he was scheduled to attend the meeting and was not present only because he was unexpectedly called away for talks with an important international figure.[95]

UN military officials described the attack against Aideed's headquarters as a "complete success." One senior official called it "a very heavy hit on the SNA leadership. ... They're stunned."[96] But the effects were, in fact, short lived. Rather than "crippling the SNA," the strike "merely caused a brief period of disarray before the SNA regrouped with new leaders."[97]

More important, instead of weakening Aideed's power base, the raid greatly strengthened it. The attack generated intense bitterness among many Somalis toward U.S. and UN forces. Indeed, the raid turned out to be a defining event in the UNOSOM II peace operation, as it "affected Somali attitudes as much as the attack on the Pakistanis had influenced attitudes within UNOSOM."[98] Anger was now directed toward other foreigners as well. Mobs turned on four journalists whom the SNA had invited to view the attack scene and beat them to death.[99]

---

[93]The International Committee of the Red Cross put the number of casualties at 54 killed and 161 wounded. See Richburg (1993), and Hirsch and Oakley (1995), p. 121, note 18.

[94]Lorch (1993a), p. A6.

[95]Drysdale (1994), p. 203.

[96]Lorch (1993a).

[97]Hirsch and Oakley (1995), p. 121, note 17.

[98]Hirsch and Oakley (1995), p. 121.

[99]Donatella Lorch "U.N. Finds Peace Elusive with Somali Leader at Large," *New York Times,* July 15, 1993b, p. A10, and Lorch (1993a).

The strike also increased Somali support for Aideed at a time when his hold on power was less than robust. Other leaders within Aideed's Habr Gidr subclan had been close to running him out of town on several occasions. But as one observer put it:

> Each time he was rescued, inadvertently, by the United States, Aideed deftly learned that he could unite his forces only by focusing on a common enemy; a call to arms against infidels and imperialists still gets adrenaline pumping in that part of Africa.[100]

In the view of U.S. Ambassador Robert Oakley and John Hirsch, the raid "caused a number of non–Habr Gidr to sympathize, and even join forces with, the SNA" and increased "Aideed's support among those Habr Gidr who had not previously been with him." The attack also had two additional "irrevocable" effects: It greatly diminished any chance for an accommodation between the SNA and the United States and UNOSOM II, and it led Aideed to make a calculated decision to kill Americans.[101]

According to Abdi Abshir Kahiye, a spokesman for the SNA whose father was killed in the air strike, Somalis after July 12 "tried to kill anybody American. There was no more United Nations—only Americans . . . and if you could kill Americans, it would start problems in America directly."[102] Leaflets were circulated in Mogadishu calling on Muslims worldwide to "kill Americans" and proclaiming that Somalis would now launch an attack against American compounds in the city.[103] On August 8, the SNA exploded a remote con-

---

[100]Michael Maren, "Somalia: Whose Failure?" *Current History*, May 1996, p. 203.

[101]Hirsch and Oakley (1995), pp. 121–122. In the words of a Western journalist who was stationed in Mogadishu at the time, the intended result of the raid "backfired: any wavering Somali was now full committed against the UN, since the dead were largely elders who had left their shoes at the door." See Scott Peterson, *Me Against My Brother*, New York: Routledge, 2000, p. 130.

[102]Richburg (1993). One Somali, who had "never taken up a gun throughout the war," told a Western journalist that the raid had made him "so angry" that if he had encountered an American on the day of the attack, he "would have shot him." The journalist described this Somali as "among the best-educated Somalis" he had ever met. See Peterson (2000), p. 133.

[103]The leaflets were signed by the *Muslim Voice*, a publication believed to be associated with Aideed's faction.

trol mine under a humvee, killing four U.S. troops. Six more Americans were wounded by a land mine on August 22.[104]

The Somali opposition became so animated that it eventually rendered the continued presence of U.S. forces in Mogadishu untenable. During the October 3–4, 1993, firefight between U.S. Rangers and Aideed's militia, which followed the Ranger capture of SNA leaders in Aideed's section of Mogadishu, an estimated 1,000 Somali men, women, and children suffered death or injury in suicidal attacks on the U.S. forces.[105] The American casualties taken in this battle—18 killed and 75 wounded—greatly intensified the growing public and congressional opposition to the U.S. involvement in Somalia and prompted President Clinton to announce that all U.S. forces would be withdrawn from the country by March 31, 1994.[106]

DIRECT ATTACKS FREQUENTLY FAIL TO NEUTRALIZE THEIR INTENDED TARGETS

Direct attacks on enemy leaders by external powers are rarely successful. The only successful U.S.-conducted or -orchestrated elimination of a major enemy leader by direct attack was the shoot-down of Admiral Yamamoto in 1943.

There is conflicting evidence as to whether American-supplied weapons may have been used in the shooting of Rafael Trujillo in May 1961, but the U.S. role in the Dominican leader's assassination seems to have been largely indirect.[107] The repeated U.S. plots to kill

---

[104]Hirsch and Oakley (1995), p. 122.

[105]Conservative counts put the number of Somali dead at 500. See Mark Bowden, *Black Hawk Down*, New York: Atlantic Monthly Press, 1999, p. 333.

[106]Richburg (1993). See also Eric V. Larson, *Casualties and Consensus*, Santa Monica, Calif.: RAND, MR-726-RC, 1996, pp. 67–72.

[107]The United States generally supported the Dominican dissidents who shot Trujillo, and some U.S. personnel were aware that the dissidents intended to kill Trujillo. American officials furnished three pistols and three carbines to the dissidents, but "there is conflicting evidence concerning whether the weapons were knowingly supplied for use in the assassination and whether any of them were present at the scene." The U.S. Senate investigation of alleged assassination plots also concluded that there was no direct U.S. involvement in the killings of Patrice Lumumba (Congo/Zaire) in 1961, Ngo Dinh Diem (South Vietnam) in 1963, and General Rene Schneider (Chile) in 1970. See U.S. Senate, *Alleged Assassination Plots Involving Foreign Leaders: An*

Castro between 1960 and 1965 all failed. More recent U.S. attempts to capture Aideed in Somalia and neutralize Qaddafi, Saddam, bin Laden, and Milosevic by air or cruise missile attack have also proved unsuccessful.

Such leaders are hard to kill because they devote careful attention to their personal security, and some have survived numerous coup and assassination attempts. They habitually maintain tight security about their planned movements and change locations frequently, conducting state business from a variety of safe houses and other sites and seldom sleeping more than a few nights at the same residence.[108]

At time of heightened peril, these leaders become even more peripatetic or seek protection in underground bunkers. In the weeks prior to the U.S. invasion of Panama, Noriega is said to have moved to different locations an average of five times a night.[109] Qaddafi is said to have escaped injury from U.S. attacks because he was located in an underground bunker at the time of the U.S. bombing. Qaddafi—fearing another U.S. aerial strike or a U.S.-prompted assassination attempt—abandoned his bunker and headquarters at Azziziyah Barracks compound and moved around Libya aboard an armored bus during the months immediately following the U.S. air attack.

The Case of Saddam Hussein

Saddam, correctly assuming that residential areas would be off limits to Coalition air attacks, apparently relocated to a residential section of Baghdad even before the Gulf War bombing began.[110] The private homes he used for refuge were chosen specifically for their innocent appearance and were rarely slept in for more than one night.

Interim Report of the Select Committee to Study Government Operations, Washington, D.C.: U.S. Government Printing Office, 1975, pp. 4–5.

[108]Watts et al. (1993b), p. 277; Schumacher (1986/1987), p. 336; and Martin and Walcott (1988), p. 296.

[109]Thomas Donnelly, Margaret Roth, and Caleb Baker, *Operation Just Cause*, New York: Lexington Books, 1991, p. 105.

[110]William H. Arkin, "Baghdad: The Urban Sanctuary in Desert Storm?" *Airpower Journal*, Spring 1997, and Atkinson (1993).

Saddam's meetings with Yevgeni Primakov, the Soviet official whom Gorbachev sent to Baghdad to broker peace between Iraq and the Coalition, and with CNN correspondent Peter Arnett all took place in houses located in Baghdad residential areas.[111]

To escape attack, Saddam sometimes used American-made Wander-lodge recreational vehicles for staff conferences and travel.[112] For camouflage, he also used a lorry and an old taxicab to move about Baghdad. According to General Wafic Al Samarrai, former head of Iraqi military intelligence:

> Saddam never frequented the well-known palaces all during the war. He moved in the city center and moved out to the outskirts but he was quite well away from the places where there was shelling. I think the nearest they got was ten kilometers from where he actually was. Saddam personally did not have any particular bunker for himself. There are many bunkers in Baghdad. Some of these are for command and control. Some of them are located under the presidential palace. One of them is in al Amariya, which was hit by U.S. aircraft and it claimed many lives.

> He frequented all these bunkers . . . also many of these bunkers were built recently to protect people against nuclear attacks. He did not come to these bunkers to sleep in them. He preferred to sleep in very usual, normal civilian houses.[113]

It is also possible that, at some point during the bombing campaign, Saddam occupied facilities that were later struck. He may even have experienced one or more near misses, but we have no definitive evidence of this.

In contrast with General Samarrai's claim that Coalition strikes never got closer than ten kilometers from Saddam, GEN Norman

---

[111]Saddam met with Arnett on January 28 and with Primakov on February 12, 1991. See Yevgeni Primakov, "My Final Visit with Saddam Hussein," *Time*, March 11, 1991, p. 44, and Robert D. McFadden, "Hussein Hints Use of All His Weapons," *New York Times*, January 29, 1991, p. A12.

[112]Barry D. Watts et al., *Gulf War Air Power Survey (GWAPS)*, Vol. II: *Operations and Effects and Effectiveness*, Part I: *Operations*, Washington, D.C.: U.S. Government Printing Office, 1993a, p. 241.

[113]See *Frontline*'s interview with General Samarrai ("The Gulf War," *Frontline*, PBS, January 28, 1997).

Schwarzkopf reports that Saddam barely escaped death when Coalition aircraft struck a large convoy in which he was riding: "It is my understanding that we hit the vehicle in front of his and the vehicle behind his and killed the bodyguards in it [but] didn't touch him."[114]

In at least one instance, Saddam seems to have evaded attack because of the Coalition's concern to avoid civilian casualties. Gen Charles Horner, the Coalition Air Component commander, reports that in the final days of the war air planners got "very good" intelligence about the location of Saddam. However, the target was located in a residential area of Baghdad, which would have caused "widespread collateral damage."[115]

The Cases of Noriega and Aideed

Even with substantial U.S. forces on the ground, it has proved difficult to locate and capture leaders such as Manuel Noriega and Mohamed Aideed in urban settings. Noriega, who was knowledgeable about U.S. intelligence techniques as a result of his training in U.S. military intelligence schools, proved particularly adept at using deceptive measures to escape U.S. monitoring. Noriega's capture was a priority objective of Operation Just Cause and in the weeks prior to the U.S. invasion, the U.S. Southern Command (SOUTHCOM) maintained an around-the-clock "Noriega watch" on the Panamanian leader's daily activities and routes.[116] A cell of watchers at SOUTHCOM monitored radio and telephone communications relating to Noriega's whereabouts and directed a network of U.S.- and Panamanian-manned surveillance teams that tracked Noriega's movements. However, the false messages and decoy convoys routinely used to mask Noriega's whereabouts caused the U.S. surveillance teams to lose track of the Panamanian leader just prior to the U.S. invasion. Thereafter, despite an intensive U.S. manhunt that barely missed apprehending Noriega on several occasions, the Panamanian leader managed to elude capture until he took refuge in the papal nunciature four days after the U.S. attack.[117]

---

[114]See *Frontline's* interview with General Schwarzkopf ("The Gulf War," 1997).

[115]See *Frontline's* interview with General Horner ("The Gulf War," 1997).

[116]Donnelly, Roth, and Baker (1991), p. 104.

[117]Donnelly, Roth, and Baker (1991), pp. 104–113.

General Aideed in Somalia proved an even more difficult subject to locate and capture. Despite continuous U.S. helicopter surveillance of Mogadishu and an intensive focus of other U.S. intelligence assets on determining his whereabouts, the wily Somali leader was able to elude capture during the entirety of the abortive U.S. and UN three-month-long "hunt for Aideed."

To avoid detection, Aideed reportedly changed his location once or twice a night and adopted disguises and other deceptive tactics, including the planting of false information about his planned movements. Only two or three of his closest aides knew his whereabouts. To further bolster his personal security, Aideed reorganized his intelligence network and weeded out suspected double agents thought to be in the pay of the UN or the CIA. American commanders nevertheless claimed that U.S. forces had Aideed in their "gunsights at least twice" during the hunt but that the "goal was not to kill" the Somali leader.[118]

PREREQUISITES OF EFFECTIVE AIR ATTACKS ON ENEMY LEADERS

Accurate, Up-to-Date Intelligence

To effectively attack senior enemy leaders, air campaign planners will require accurate, up-to-date human (HUMINT) and other intelligence on the location of these leaders at a given time. They will also require the capability to strike targets effectively within the window provided by this intelligence.

Because wary leaders like Saddam Hussein frequently change location to foil assassination plots or military attacks, air planners will probably require either predictive or near-real-time intelligence on the whereabouts of their leadership targets. Acquiring such information will prove difficult in the types of closed, security-conscious regimes that the United States is most likely to confront.

Predictive intelligence will be needed if time is required to mount an attack. When commenting on the Coalition's failure to hit Saddam

---

[118]See Peterson (2000), pp. 96–98.

during the Gulf War, Harry E. Soyster, the Army general who headed the Defense Intelligence Agency during the bombing campaign, said,

> You can find out, perhaps, where he has been. You can find out even where he is. But what you need to know is where he's going to be because you must mount an attack. And so it's almost an impossible task.[119]

Buster Glosson, the Air Force general who planned the Gulf War air campaign, indicated that a lack of HUMINT limited the Coalition's ability to locate Saddam:

> There is no question it is tough to determine an enemy's intentions without some HUMINT. It's next to impossible to determine someone's location using only technical intelligence. If you don't have HUMINT as a fail-safe [or] sanity check, you find yourself boxing with a lot of shadows.[120]

The U.S. hunt for Aideed in Somalia was also greatly hampered by a lack of predictive intelligence and reliable HUMINT. General Joseph Hoar, Commander, U.S. Central Command (CENTCOM), saw a

> real problem with HUMINT. The people who provided information lacked credibility. . . . I felt the possibility of getting predictive intelligence regarding Aideed was poor; it was. But we did everything favorable to produce the intelligence.[121]

It should be noted that the one U.S. success—the shoot-down of Admiral Yamamoto's aircraft in 1943—was based on predictive intelligence. The attack was made possible by the decryption of messages concerning the admiral's itinerary, which the Japanese had sent out from Rabaul on New Britain Island to alert subordinate units about the admiral's visit to their various commands.[122]

---

[119]See "The Gulf War" (1997).

[120]David A. Fulghum, "Glosson: U.S. Gulf War Shortfalls Linger," *Aviation Week & Space Technology*, January 29, 1996, p. 58.

[121]General Hoar's view about the shortcomings of HUMINT in Somalia was shared by the other U.S. commanders associated with the hunt for Aideed. See Senator John Warner and Senator Carl Levin, "Memorandum for Senator Thurmond and Senator Nunn," Washington, D.C.: U.S. Senate Committee on Armed Services, September 29, 1995, p. 42.

[122]See Spector (1985), pp. 227–228, and Agawa (1979), pp. 369–379.

Special Munitions for Some Targets

Special munitions may be required if the United States is to success-fully attack enemy leaders in some future conflict situations. In the case of another war with North Korea, for example, a large inventory of penetrating weapons would be needed to attack effectively the numerous leadership and C^3 sites that are located deep underground throughout that country. In conflicts where enemy leaders seek refuge from the bombing in civilian residential areas, extremely accurate low-yield munitions will be required to attack such leader-ship sites without causing large-scale civilian casualties or collateral damage.

Assurances That the Attack Will Be Legal and Beneficial If Successful

Finally, any deliberate attack against an enemy leader must, of course, be in keeping with the international law of armed conflict and Executive Order 12333. Decisionmakers must also determine that the likely benefits of the attack will outweigh its likely costs. In making this judgment, decisionmakers will have to try to assess pos-sible longer-term consequences as well as the likely short-term effects.

Possible unintended consequences are likely to prove particularly difficult to assess. However, as with the physician, the decision-maker's first concern should be to avoid doing harm. To help his evaluation of potential downside consequences, the decisionmaker should consult the views of area experts knowledgeable about the enemy country and its leadership.[123]

---

[123]Gen Charles Horner, the Coalition air commander during the 1991 Persian Gulf War, commented in an interview that even though stealth and precision technologies had allowed the United States to attack targets in heavily defended urban areas,

> what we haven't learned is how to exploit this revolutionary capability. . . . I think we learned we need to do a better job of analysis of target systems, such as [enemy] "leadership" [sites] in order to have effective attacks, and I do not believe we are strong in the area of understanding other cultures, modes of leadership, and the ways to alter them so as to fit our goals and objectives in a war.

See the *Washington Post* interview with General Horner, "Fog of War" (1998).

It will be important that the decisionmaker understand how a successful leadership attack might affect popular attitudes both within the country and in the world at large, its probable impact on the sources of the enemy policy and behavior the United States finds injurious to its interests, and how it would most likely affect the inner power relationships within the enemy camp. Particular emphasis should be given to identifying and establishing the likely policy orientation of the targeted leader's probable successor.

Chapter Three

FACILITATING COUPS OR REBELLIONS

ASSUMPTIONS UNDERLYING SUPPORT TO COUPS OR REBELLIONS

The United States might also act to remove or intimidate hostile leaders by attempting to facilitate their overthrow by a coup or rebellion. In sanctioning military and other support to a coup or rebellion, U.S. decisionmakers might anticipate consequences such as the following:

- U.S. assistance would be sufficient to make an otherwise problematic coup or rebellion successful.

- The successor government installed after the overthrow would adopt policies and behavior more acceptable to the United States.

- Even if the hostile regime was not overthrown, the regime's perception of the threats posed by continued coup plotting or by a U.S.-supported rebel force would provide the United States with bargaining leverage.

- In the event that U.S. forces became engaged in combat with the forces of the enemy regime, any enemy resources diverted to guard against a threatened coup or rebellion would weaken the enemy's frontline fighting capabilities.

A POOR SUCCESS RATE WITH COUPS AND REBELLIONS

During the course of the Cold War, the United States supported coups and rebellions in an attempt to prevent countries with left-leaning regimes from moving decisively into the USSR's orbit; backed resistance movements in countries occupied by external communist forces; and attempted to generate rebellions in Third World states already ruled by Marxist-Leninist governments. During the 1980s and 1990s, the United States also attempted to unseat leaders who were viewed as promoting policies threatening to U.S. interests. With a few notable exceptions, such U.S. attempts to remove undesirable leaders by coup or rebellion have failed.

A Few Weakly Protected Governments Were Ousted

During the 1950s, the United States, with only minimal investment, succeeded in unseating leftist regimes in Iran and Guatemala that lacked strong support from their own military. In 1963, the United States acquiesced in the overthrow of President Ngo Dinh Diem in South Vietnam, an act that unexpectedly proved seriously counterproductive to the immediate war effort in that country.

The Overthrow of Mossadeq in Iran. In 1953, Kermit Roosevelt and a few other CIA operatives organized a successful coup against Iranian Prime Minister Mohammad Mossadeq, whom the United States saw as becoming increasingly alienated from the West and more closely allied with Iran's Soviet-dominated Tudeh Party. To prepare the way for the coup, Roosevelt eventually secured the reluctant support of the shah (who signed *firmans* [royal decrees] dismissing Mossadeq and appointing Gen. Fazlollah A. Zahedi, a high-ranking officer who had been selected to spearhead the coup, as prime minister) and that of influential mullahs and key military leaders. Roosevelt also recruited a number of Iranian agents, including some who had formerly been in the employ of the British Secret Intelligence Service, which was involved in the planning of the coup.[1]

---

[1] The most definitive account to the 1953 coup, code-named Operation TPAJAX, is the history written by Dr. Donald N. Wilber who was one of the leading CIA planners of the coup. See Donald N. Wilber, *Clandestine Service History: Overthrow of Premier Mossadeq of Iran, November 1952–August 1953*, March 1954. A summary of the history was published in James Risen "How a Plot Convulsed Iran in '53 (and in '79)," *New York Times*, April 16, 2000. pp. 1, 16, and 17. For other accounts of the coup, see Mark Gasiorowski, "The 1953 Coup d'État in Iran," *International Journal of Middle East Studies*, Vol. 19, 1987, pp. 261–286; Kermit Roosevelt, *Countercoup: The Struggle for the Control of Iran*, New York: McGraw-Hill Book Company, 1979; Stephen E. Ambrose, *Ike's Spies: Eisenhower and the Espionage Establishment*, Garden City, N.Y.: Doubleday & Company, 1981, pp. 189–214; Gregory F. Treverton, *Covert Action: The*

To prepare the groundwork for the coup, CIA agents mounted political action campaigns armed at discrediting both the Tudeh Party and the Mossadeq regime. To stir up anticommunist and antigovernment sentiment in the religious community, local CIA operatives pretending to be Tudeh Party members threatened Muslim leaders with "savage punishment if they opposed Mossadeq."[2]

The coup, which was scheduled to take place on August 16, 1953, almost came asunder when an indiscreet Iranian officer involved in the operation inadvertently betrayed the plot. The Mossadeq government took immediate preemptive action, positioning units from the Tehran garrison at key points around the city and arresting Iranian officers thought to be involved in the plot. Fortunately for the coup plotters, the Mossadeq government then played into the CIA's hands first by dissolving the parliament, which inflamed public opinion against the regime, and second by prematurely recalling most of the troops it had stationed around the city, erroneously believing that the coup plotters had been suppressed.[3]

As a result of the government broadcasts disclosing the coup plot, thousands of Tudeh partisans and other extremists took to the streets on August 15 denouncing both the shah and all Americans.[4] Washington considered this anti-American outburst sufficiently threatening to order Roosevelt to cancel his operation and pull out of Iran.[5] The Tudeh rioters, however, also overplayed their hand by "looting everything they could grab," defiling statues of the monarch, and erecting their own flags. Hoping to inflame anti-Tudeh sentiments even more, CIA political action assets feigning to be Tudehites also took to the streets to loot and smash shops.[6] The rioting contin-

---

Limits of Intervention in the Postwar World, New York: Basic Books, Inc., 1987, *passim*; and John Prados, *Presidents' Secret Wars*, Revised and Expanded Edition, Chicago: Ivan R. Dee, 1986, pp. 91, 98.

[2]Risen (2000), p. 16.

[3]Wilber (1954), p. 53, and Risen (2000), p. 17.

[4]See Ambrose (1981), p. 208.

[5]The Washington message to withdraw, which was sent through Cyprus by Under Secretary of State Walter Bedell Smith, was held up by the British and did not reach Roosevelt until after the coup had succeeded. Roosevelt disclosed that the Tudeh rioting had "scared the hell out" of him as well. Ambrose (1981), pp. 208, 210.

[6]See Wilber (1954), pp. 62–63.

ued for two days and was quelled only after the U.S. ambassador to Iran, Loy Henderson, cajoled Mossadeq into ordering his U.S.-trained police to restore order. Henderson had threatened to pull all Americans out of the country if the rioting did not stop—a contingency Mossadeq found unacceptable in that it would "make it appear that his government could not govern." Stephen Ambrose characterized Mossadeq's agreement to crack down on his Tudeh allies as the "old man's fatal mistake." Policemen and soldiers previously constrained from taking steps that might offend the Tudeh "were delighted to be turned loose."[7]

With the Tudeh rioters forcibly dispersed and subdued, Roosevelt's Iranian agents swung into action. They arranged for copies of the shah's *firmans* dismissing Mossadeq and appointing Zahedi to be widely disseminated throughout Tehran in newspapers and hand-delivered broadsheets.[8] They also undertook to purchase a mob of their own to demonstrate this time in support for the Shah. On August 19, 1953, a pro-Shah demonstration began to form in Tehran's bazaar area and rapidly took on "overwhelming proportions." Even though some CIA political action assets were involved in its incitement, the demonstration was largely spontaneous. Army troops and armored elements soon joined the demonstrators. Still-at-large Iranian military leaders involved in the coup who had heretofore been dormant swung into action, directing their forces to seize key government facilities and arrest progovernment military and civilian officials.[9] Pro-shah military units armed with tanks moved on Mossadeq's house and in a two-hour battle subdued the troops of Mossadeq's household guard, who surrendered once their ammunition ran out. Total casualties to both sides in this battle—which constituted the only organized fighting during the coup—were estimated at 100 killed and 300 wounded.[10] By the end of the day, the country was in the hands of a new premier, General Zahedi, and

---

[7]According to an eyewitness account by *New York Times* correspondent Kenneth Love, "The troops appeared to be in a frenzy as they smashed into the rioters with clubbed rifles and nightsticks, and hurled teargas bombs." Ambrose (1981), p. 209.

[8]Wilber (1954), p. 65.

[9]The coup plotters had developed "arrest lists" of the Mossadeq officials and supporters to be detained. See Wilber (1954), pp. xii, 65–74, and Appendix D, pp. 6–7.

[10]Ambrose (1981), p. 211.

members of the Mossadeq government were either in hiding or incarcerated.[11]

The entire operation to overthrow Mossadeq "from first order to end" took but six months and probably cost $1 million dollars or so, including the $200,000 Roosevelt reportedly spent to finance anti-Mossadeq street demonstrations.[12] According to Roosevelt, the coup succeeded because Mossadeq lacked support both within the Iranian military and among the public at large. As Roosevelt saw it, when the people and the armed forces were shown that they had to choose between the monarch and a revolutionary figure backed by the former Soviet Union, "the people and the army came, overwhelmingly, to the support of the Shah." The British officials who were closely involved in the coup planning estimated that, whereas only a few top army leaders were probably pro-Mossadeq, the "bulk of the officers and essentially all noncoms and enlisted personnel" were loyal to the shah.[13]

The Overthrow of Arbenz in Guatemala. Emboldened by the success of the Iranian operation, the CIA orchestrated a combination of military and psychological pressures to drive the leftist Guatemalan president, Jacobo Arbenz, from office in 1954. The operation, code-named Operation BPSUCCESS, employed an invasion by a ragtag "liberation" army, psychologically effective CIA air attacks, fictional arms drops, and disinformation disseminated over a CIA-controlled "Voice of Liberation" radio to prompt leaders of the Guatemalan army to demand the president's resignation.[14] The CIA operation succeeded despite the fact that it was plagued by chronic lapses in security; inadequate planning; a poor understanding of the inten-

---

[11]Wilber (1954), p. xii.

[12]See Treverton (1987), pp. 45 and 267, note 3, and Wilber (1954), p. 3.

[13]See Roosevelt (1979), pp. 119–121, 161–210.

[14]For differing accounts of the operation, see Stephen Schlesinger, and Stephen Kinzer, *Bitter Fruit: The Untold Story of the American Coup in Guatemala*, New York: Doubleday & Company, Inc., 1982; Richard H. Immerman, *The CIA in Guatemala: The Foreign Policy of Intervention*, Austin, Tex.: University of Texas Press, 1997.; Nick Cullather, *Secret History: The CIA's Classified Account of Its Operations in Guatemala 1952–1954*, Stanford, Calif.: Stanford University Press, 1999; Piero Gleijeses, *Shattered Hope: The Guatemalan Revolution and the United States, 1944–1954*, Princeton, N.J.: Princeton University Press, 1991, pp. 279–387; Prados (1986), pp. 98–107; Treverton (1987), *passim*; and Ambrose (1981), pp. 224–234.

tions of the Guatemalan army, the Arbenz government, and its political allies; and the "hopeless weakness" of the friendly forces that had been recruited to invade the country.[15]

The CIA-supported invasion that was launched from neighboring Honduras on June 20, 1954, under the overall command of Arbenz's intended successor, Colonel Carlos Castillo Armas, ran into immediate trouble when two of its four prongs were decisively defeated by small government police and army elements acting on their own initiative. These setbacks cost Armas almost half of his initial 480-man army. The remainder of Armas's forces eventually penetrated some 30 miles into the country, occupying several towns that surrendered essentially without a fight. However, even when bolstered by additional recruits, the invasion force could easily have been crushed by the government troops situated in the local area, had the Guatemalan army commanders chosen to attack them.[16]

The Guatemalan military leaders opted not to fight because they were paralyzed by the fear that the United States, if need be, would intervene with its own forces to oust Arbenz. As one Guatemalan officer explained: "Fear defeated them. They were terrorized by the idea that the United States was looming behind Castillo Armas."[17] To foreclose the possibility of such a military confrontation with the United States, the senior Guatemalan military leaders decided that Arbenz must resign.[18] Following a "game of musical chairs" in which five provisional governments, each entirely staffed by military officers, succeeded one another, the United States finally maneuvered Armas into the presidency on July 7, 1954.[19]

The Overthrow of Diem in South Vietnam. In 1963, senior officials in the Kennedy administration concluded that South Vietnamese President Ngo Dinh Diem was hindering the successful prosecution of the counterinsurgency war in South Vietnam and had to be replaced. A group of anti-Diem Army of Vietnam (ARVN) generals began plotting against the South Vietnamese president with the

---

[15]Cullather (1999), p. 97.

[16]See Cullather (1999), pp. 89–92, 109.

[17]Quoted in Gleijeses (1991), p. 338.

[18]Gleijeses (1991), pp. 345–346.

[19]Gleijeses (1991), pp. 351–357.

"active acquiescence" of U.S. officials in Saigon and Washington. On October 6, 1963, U.S. Ambassador Henry Cabot Lodge received the following instruction from Washington:

> While we do not wish to stimulate a coup, we also do not wish to leave the impression that U.S. would thwart a change of government or deny economic and military assistance to a new regime if it appeared capable of increasing effectiveness of military effort, ensuring popular support to win the war and improving relations with the U.S.[20]

As a former senior officer in the CIA's clandestine service put it: "No attempt was made to stop the coup and in effect American officials gave the generals a green light."[21]

The ARVN forces that spearheaded the coup on November 1 rapidly overwhelmed Diem's palace guard. Diem and his brother Nhu eluded capture for a few days but were eventually taken into custody and killed by junior ARVN officers. American officials had wanted Diem to be given safe conduct out of the country and were shocked by his execution.

The coup produced serious unintended consequences. Rather than facilitate the counterinsurgency effort in South Vietnam as the U.S. officials had expected, the removal of Diem further undermined it. Diem's overthrow, as one historian put it, "did not lead to a regime more responsive to the needs of the people of South Vietnam and it brought with it a dangerous degree of political instability."[22] A series of power struggles and further leadership changes ensued, producing governments that were neither particularly popular nor competent. The turmoil in Saigon and the changes in provincial leadership that followed each governmental turnover significantly disrupted South Vietnamese efforts to secure the areas of the countryside, where the Viet Cong were actively contesting government control.[23] Indeed, emboldened by the diversions in Saigon, the "Viet Cong made

---

[20]Guenter Lewy, *America in Vietnam*, New York: Oxford University Press, 1978, p. 27.

[21]Harry Rositzke, *CIA's Secret Operations*, New York: Reader's Digest Press, 1977, p. 202.

[22]Lewy (1978), p. 28.

[23]Lewy (1978), p. 28.

widespread political and military advances across the country, and many of the Strategic Hamlets were overrun."[24]

Most Attempts to Oust Entrenched Regimes Have Failed

Balanced against the successes in Iran and Guatemala is a longer list of instances over the past 50 years in which U.S. attempts to foment successful coups and rebellions against more entrenched regimes failed. These include the U.S. attempts to overthrow Enver Hoxa in Albania, Fidel Castro in Cuba, Muammar al-Qaddafi in Libya, Manuel Noriega in Panama, and Saddam Hussein in Iraq.

The Attempt to Unseat the Hoxa Regime in Albania. In spring 1950, the United Kingdom and the United States made a concerted effort to organize a guerrilla movement in Albania that would gain enough popular support to overthrow the communist government in Tirana. Albania had become an attractive target for paramilitary action because the Hoxa regime's control appeared to be somewhat shaky. Over a period of two years, British and American agents attempted to infiltrate team after team of "free Albanians" into the country by air, sea, and land. However, none of these teams succeeded in gaining a foothold, as all were betrayed beforehand:

> Almost every mission misfired. Teams sent across the border from Greece ran into police ambushes. Teams landing from rubber craft were met at the beach by police. Drop zones were surrounded by Albanian troops. A few radio operators who came up on the air transmitted under Albanian control.[25]

The armed "liberation" of Albania proved to be a disaster. The operation had been thoroughly compromised from the start by Kim Philby, a Soviet agent, who oversaw the London desk of the British service that ran the clandestine Albanian operations. Philby not only informed Moscow of British-American plans but also provided details on the dispatch of individual agent teams before they landed in Albania.[26]

---

[24]Phillip B. Davidson, *Vietnam at War*, Novato, Calif.: Presidio Press, 1988, p. 303.

[25]Rositzke (1977), p. 172.

[26]Rositzke (1977), p. 172.

The Attempts to Overthrow the Castro Regime in Cuba. On April 17, 1961, the CIA sponsored the landing of some 1,500 combat-trained and heavily armed Cuban exiles at the Bay of Pigs along the southern coast of Cuba. This brigade-sized force was expected to maintain itself in Cuba for a sufficient period of time "to administer a 'shock' and thereby, it was hoped, to trigger an uprising" and defections from Castro's armed forces.[27] As the CIA's inspector general described it in his critique of the Bay of Pigs operation:

> The invasion operation was based on the hope that the brigade would be able to maintain itself in Cuba long enough to prevail by attracting insurgents and defectors from the Castro armed services, but without having in advance any assurance of assistance from identified, known, controlled, trained, and organized guerrillas. The Agency hoped the invasion would, like a *deus ex machina*, produce a "shock," which would cause these defections. In other words ... the invasion was to take the place of an organized resistance which did not exist and was to generate organized resistance by providing the focus and acting as a catalyst.[28]

The inspector general found such expectations unrealistic given the failure of the CIA's earlier attempt to supply the nascent Cuban resistance groups by airdrops and "the success of the Castro security forces in arresting our agents, rolling up the few existing nets, and reducing guerrilla groups to ineffectiveness." Indeed, following the D-day-minus-2 air strike that preceded the invasion, Castro's security forces immediately arrested some "tens of thousands of suspected persons." The inspector general also found it unrealistic to expect a 1,500-man brigade, put ashore by amphibious landing, to prevail over a revolutionary army of some 32,000 men and a militia of some 200,000 men armed with communist bloc heavy weapons.[29]

---

[27]See the CIA inspector general's critique of the Bay of Pigs operation for the Director of Central Intelligence in CIA, *Survey of the Cuban Operation and Associated Documents*, Washington, D.C., February 16, 1962, p. 47. For the official critique of the Bay of Pigs operation, conducted by the Cuban Study Group chaired by General Maxwell D. Taylor, see Board of Inquiry on the Bay of Pigs, *Operation Zapata: The "Ultrasensitive" Report and Testimony of the Board of Inquiry on the Bay of Pigs*, Frederick, Md.: Aletheia Books, University Publications of America, Inc., 1981.

[28]CIA (1962), p. 54.

[29]CIA (1962), pp. 54–56.

An important component of the Bay of Pigs operation was the plan to neutralize Castro's air force. On April 15, eight B-26s flown from a CIA base in Nicaragua destroyed approximately half of Cuba's combat aircraft. However, late on April 16, the eve of D day, the air strikes designed to destroy the rest of Castro's air force on the following morning were canceled. When the CIA's cover story about the origins of the first strike began to unravel—the legend was that the B-26s were from Castro's own air force and were piloted by defectors—Secretary of State Dean Rusk and President John Kennedy concluded that "a second strike from Nicaragua would raise the international noise level to an intolerable degree."[30] As a result, Castro's remaining T-33 jets, Sea Furies, and B-26s were eventually able both to prevent the invasion force from being resupplied from the sea and to reduce greatly the interdiction and close support the invasion force could receive from friendly B-26s. The absence of ammunition resupply and the fact that the terrain in the Bay of Pigs area offered little possibility for a breakout doomed the surrounded exile brigade to catastrophic defeat.[31]

In November 1961, the United States initiated a major new covert action program to overthrow Castro. Code-named "Operation Mongoose," the program initially sought to use propaganda and sabotage to create the conditions whereby the Cuban "people themselves would overthrow the Castro regime."[32] However, a growing realization that the Castro regime was unlikely to be overturned by internal means without direct U.S. military intervention led U.S. planners in August 1962 to change the overall objective of Operation Mongoose from one of overthrowing the Castro regime to one of causing its failure by splitting off Castro from "old-line communists."[33] In 1963, the objective of the U.S. covert action programs was downgraded once again to the even more limited aim of nourishing "a spirit of resistance and disaffection which could lead to significant defection and other by-products of unrest."[34] However, there is little evidence

---

[30]Peter Wyden, *Bay of Pigs*, New York: Simon and Schuster, 1979, pp. 198–199.

[31]CIA (1962), pp. 28–33, 55.

[32]See U.S. Senate (1975), pp. 139–140.

[33]U.S. Senate (1975), p. 163.

[34]U.S. Senate (1975), p. 173.

that U.S. covert operations were able to secure even this modest objective on an island a mere 90 miles from the U.S. coast.

The Attempts to Spark a Coup in Libya.   When Qaddafi began to challenge American interests in the early 1970s, U.S. agencies were asked to increase attention on collecting intelligence on "Libya, Qaddafi's machinations, and the activities of Libyan groups opposed to Qaddafi."[35]   After the Reagan administration assumed power in 1981, the United States began to pursue Qaddafi's overthrow assertively, establishing contacts with various Libyan opposition groups in both Rome and Cairo. By mid-1981, President Reagan had directed that "nonlethal" aid and training be provided to some anti-Qaddafi exiles.[36]   American officials also reportedly explored the possibility of joint covert operations against Qaddafi with representatives from several other countries, including Egypt and France.[37]

In spring 1982, the Reagan administration initiated measures designed to exploit Qaddafi's political vulnerabilities and "create the conditions for an internal military coup."[38]   A proposal for more potent U.S. action to topple Qaddafi surfaced in fall 1985, when President Reagan signed an intelligence finding authorizing the CIA to provide lethal aid to the Libyan opposition groups undergoing training in Egypt and Algeria. However, this covert plan ran into opposition from leaders of the U.S. Senate Intelligence Committee and had to be scuttled when it was leaked to the *Washington Post*.[39]

Although the central purpose of the April 1986 air strikes on Libya was to send a message to Qaddafi about the price he would pay if he continued to support terrorism, Washington decisionmakers apparently also hoped that the air attacks might help promote a coup or, eventually, some kind of popular uprising against Qaddafi. Within minutes after the U.S. bombs had fallen, the Voice of America's

---

[35]One of the CIA's key listening posts was Rome, which "was awash in Libyans"— Libya having been a former colony of Italy. See Duane R. Clarridge, *A Spy for All Seasons: My Life in the CIA*, New York: Scribner, 1997, pp. 174–175.

[36]Clarridge (1997), pp. 174–175, and Stanik (1996), p. 7.

[37]Leslie H. Gelb, "U.S. Official Reports Contact with Qaddafi Foes," *New York Times*, April 17, 1986, p. A24.

[38]Stanik (1996), p. 11.

[39]Stanik (1996), p. 13, and Martin and Walcott (1988), p. 266.

Libyan service began repeated broadcasts of an editorial pointing out the tragic costs to the Libyan people of Qaddafi's continued rule.[40] In a speech following the raid, President Reagan took pains to distinguish between America's quarrel with Qaddafi and its sympathy toward a people "caught in the grip of a tyrant."[41] The obvious import of the message was that Libya could expect good relations with the United States once Qaddafi was ousted.[42]

Whereas Reagan administration officials probably thought the likelihood of a popular uprising in Libya to be low, they seemed to have harbored greater expectations about the possibility of a coup. At his news conference on the day following the attack, Secretary of State George Shultz disclosed that the targets of the air strikes, including the attacks on the Azziziyah Barracks compound that housed Qaddafi's personal guard unit, were selected, at least in part, to stimulate anti-Qaddafi action by the Libyan military. Expressing the belief that "there was considerable dissidence in the armed forces of Libya with Qaddafi and what he is doing," Shultz said that the United States had tried to send two messages by the targets selected for attack: First, Libya's involvement in terrorist activities was likely to cost the Libyan military some of the equipment it most prized; second, the "Praetorian Guards that surround Qaddafi and intimidate the people are not invulnerable."[43] Asked if this would encourage a coup, Shultz replied that if there is a coup,

> that's all to the good. We know there are lots of people in Libya who think Libya would be better off if Qaddafi was not there. There are even more people not in Libya who think that.[44]

---

[40]The message read: "The people of the United States bear Libya and its people no enmity or hatred. However, Colonel Qaddafi is your head of state. So long as Libyans obey his orders, then they must accept the consequences. Colonel Qaddafi is your tragic burden. The Libyan people are responsible for Colonel Qaddafi and his actions. If you permit Colonel Qaddafi to continue with the present conflict, then you must also share some collective responsibility for his actions." Quoted in Martin and Walcott (1988), p. 313.

[41]Quoted in Steven R. David, *Third World Coups d'état and International Security,* Baltimore: Johns Hopkins University Press, 1987, p. 59.

[42]David (1987), p. 59.

[43]Bernard Gwertzman, "Shultz Expresses Hopes for a Coup to Oust Qaddafi," *New York Times,* April 18, 1986, pp. A1, A10.

[44]Gwertzman (1986), p. A10.

There is no evidence that this rhetoric or the fine-tuning of military targets produced the hoped-for effect on the Libyan military. Indeed, one observer argues that rather than facilitating a coup, the raid had the opposite effect of strengthening Qaddafi vis-à-vis his potential rivals within the government.[45] According to this view, the attack ruined the chances of a military revolt because it demoralized the armed forces and discredited them in the eyes of the Libyan public: "After the attack, there was no support for a coup."[46]

At any rate, these actions and the more subtle military and covert pressure the Reagan administration subsequently applied against Libya in hopes of provoking a coup failed to produce Qaddafi's ouster. Of the many coup attempts mounted against Qaddafi during the 1980s and 1990s, it is unclear whether any were the result of U.S. activities.[47]

Qaddafi's continued survival in power can be attributed in part to the fact that Libyans are "largely apolitical people" who are known to be "wistfully peaceful, with little taste for fighting—in ironic counterpoint to their leader."[48] But Qaddafi's longevity is also a product of the care and resources he has invested in his personal safety and the security of his regime. Many of Qaddafi's personal bodyguards, for example, are recruited from his tribe, the Qaddafadam. Qaddafi has, moreover, kept the Libyan military in line by rotating its commanders to keep any one of them from accumulating too much power and by ruthlessly eliminating officers who might pose a threat.[49] To eliminate leaders and groups through which discontent might be channeled, Qaddafi has ordered the assassination of Libyan exiles overseas and has imprisoned and executed thousands of Libyans over the years—some by public hanging.[50]

In addition to his police and intelligence service, Qaddafi has relied on his so-called revolutionary committees to maintain control and

---

[45]Schumacher (1986/1987), p. 336.

[46]Schumacher (1986/1987), p. 338.

[47]David (1987), p. 58.

[48]See Schumacher (1986/1987), pp. 333, 342.

[49]Schumacher (1986/1987), pp. 331, 338.

[50]Schumacher (1986/1987), pp. 333, 342; see also Abubaker O. Altajuri, "Qaddafi: Still a Dictator," letter to the editor, *Foreign Affairs*, July/August 1999, pp. 154–155.

root out potential enemies. The committees are present in every neighborhood, factory, and government office and are manned by loyal political zealots who serve as informants and exercise powers that often supplant the police and the courts.[51] The committees also exist within the Libyan military, where they include loyalist soldiers of various ranks who perform critical functions, such as controlling access to the ammunition and weapon armories. Their presence makes organization for a successful coup difficult if not "virtually impossible."[52]

The Attempts to Promote a Coup Against Noriega in Panama. The United States began a determined effort to oust Manuel Noriega from power in February 1988 when the Panama Defense Force (PDF) commander seized control of the Panamanian government following his indictments by two federal grand juries in Florida on drug-trafficking charges.[53] An attempted coup against Noriega failed the following month, triggering a purge of nearly one-quarter of the PDF's officer corps and solidifying the Panamanian leader's hold on power. According to former Secretary of State James Baker, "With his usurpation of power and the indictment, Noriega became persona non grata to American policymakers overnight."[54]

Eschewing the use of U.S. troops to remove Noriega, the Reagan administration imposed stringent sanctions on Panama to build pressure on Noriega to leave office. The administration attempted to broker a deal whereby Noriega would permanently depart Panama in return for the withdrawal of the U.S. arrest warrants against him; U.S. guarantees not to extradite or "snatch" him from his place of exile; and promises to allow Panamanian funds held in the United States to flow out of escrow.[55] Although Noriega initially accepted these arrangements, he backed out of the deal when it ran into opposition from other PDF officers.[56]

---

[51]Schumacher (1986/1987), pp. 337–338, and Altajuri (1999), p. 154.

[52]Schumacher (1986/1987), p. 338.

[53]According to Secretary Shultz, the February 4, 1988, indictments were sought by the U.S. Department of Justice without adequate consultation with the State Department or the White House. See Shultz (1993), p. 1052.

[54]James A. Baker, III, *The Politics of Diplomacy*, New York: G. P. Putnam's Sons, 1995.

[55]Shultz (1993), pp. 1051–1079.

[56]See p. 96.

When Noriega stole the May 1989 Panamanian election, the Bush administration began active efforts to stimulate a coup against the Panamanian leader. American training exercises in Panama were significantly increased and were frequently staged in areas normally controlled by the PDF. According to Secretary Baker, this was psychological warfare: "We wanted Noriega to believe we were coming if he didn't leave first. More to the point, we also wanted to send the PDF a message; 'Noriega is the problem; either you remove him, or the U.S. military will.'"[57]

Secretary Baker also delivered a blunt message to Noriega, reiterating President Reagan's earlier warning that "the crisis will not end until you give up power."[58] In a transparent attempt to foment a coup, American officials in Panama were also instructed to deliver a similar message to their contacts within the PDF. The message conveyed by these U.S. officials emphasized that the United States had no quarrel with the Panamanian military and called on the PDF to restore its reputation—now sullied because of the army's brutalization of the Panamanian people—by joining in a partnership with the democratic opposition. The message concluded: "There will be no place in Panama for those who remain with Noriega until the end. The crisis will not be resolved until he gives up power. It can only get worse and worse."[59]

A coup, albeit not quite the one U.S. leaders had hoped for, occurred on October 3, 1989. American officials first learned that a coup was in the making on October 1, when the wife of a PDF major named Moises Giroldi made contact with an American official attached to SOUTHCOM headquarters at Quarry Heights and announced that her husband planned to execute a coup against Noriega the following day. She explained that Giroldi planned a bloodless coup, the aim being to "retire" Noriega from power in keeping with the 25-year limit Panamanian law imposed on service in the armed forces. While Giroldi did not want to "taint" his coup with direct U.S. military participation, he did require a limited amount of help from the U.S. military. Specifically, Giroldi asked that his family members be given

---

[57]Baker (1995), p. 183.

[58]Baker (1995), p. 184.

[59]Baker (1995), p. 185.

sanctuary while the coup was under way and that U.S. forces block two roads leading into Panama City that PDF units loyal to Noriega might use to mount a rescue attempt.[60]

The initial U.S. reaction to Major Giroldi's request for assistance was negative. American officials knew little about Giroldi, and the little they did know made them skeptical.[61] Giroldi was the commander of the security detail at the Commandancia, the PDF's headquarters, and was one of the key figures who had helped suppress the March 1988 coup against Noriega. He was therefore considered a Noriega loyalist.

Indeed, SOUTHCOM considered the coup report to be a hoax: a Noriega provocation designed to test or embarrass General Thurman, who had assumed command of SOUTHCOM only the previous day. Secretary of Defense Richard Cheney, GEN Colin Powell (who had also just assumed his position as chairman of the Joint Chiefs of Staff [JCS]), and the service chiefs all believed that the United States should not become involved in what had all the earmarks of a poorly organized effort.[62] Washington's skepticism increased when word was received that the coup would be delayed by a day. It was dismissed by Bush administration officials as another of the frequently rumored anti-Noriega coups that failed to materialize.[63]

---

[60]Giroldi requested blocks at the Bridge of the Americas, which would deny access to Panama City from the 6th and 7th PDF Mechanized Infantry companies, and at the entrance of Fort Amador, the joint U.S.-PDF base where the PDF's 5th Infantry Company was located. For accounts of the Giroldi coup, see Edward M. Flanagan, Jr. (LTG, USA, Ret.), *Battle for Panama*, Washington, D.C.: Brassey's Inc., 1993, pp. 27–31; Malcolm McConnell, *Just Cause*, New York: St. Martin's Press, 1991, pp. 9–13; Donnelly, Roth, and Baker (1991), pp. 67–69; Kevin Buckley, *Panama: The Whole Story*, New York: Simon and Schuster, 1991, pp. 196–208; and Baker (1995), pp. 185–188.

[61]According to General Powell, the SOUTCOM commander, GEN Max Thurman, initially reported that "We don't know anything about him [Giroldi]." General Thurman went on to suggest that the "coup seemed to be a job grievance" on the part of "disgruntled unpaid PDF soldiers." See Colin Powell, *My American Journey*, New York: Random House, 1995, p. 417. See also Baker (1995), p. 185.

[62]Baker (1995), p. 185. According to General Powell, "the whole affair sounded like amateur night." Powell (1995), p. 118.

[63]Baker (1995), p. 185.

The main exception to those wanting to do nothing was President Bush, who was more open to an active U.S. role. During an Oval Office meeting on October 2, he told his advisers: "Look, you've had me out there for the last couple of months begging these guys to start a coup. If someone's actually willing to do one, we have to help them." President Bush reiterated these sentiments on October 3, when the coup in fact began, and ordered U.S. troops to establish the two roadblocks requested by Major Giroldi.[64]

The coup turned out to be a poorly executed affair. Noriega, who had access to a telephone while he was in Major Giroldi's custody at the Commandancia, was able to call loyalist subordinates both in Panama City and in Rio Hato, some 75 miles away, to arrange his own rescue. The forces in Rio Hato commandeered Panamanian civil aircraft to fly them to Omar Torrijos Airport on the outskirts of the capital and from there moved rapidly to surround the Commandancia.[65]

Prior to the rescue, discussions were held between representatives of the coup group and SOUTHCOM about the possibility of turning Noriega over to U.S. authorities. These negotiations came to naught, however, because Major Giroldi and his cohorts wanted the political cover of having U.S. forces conspicuously seize Noriega from their custody, whereas General Thurman was ordered not to initiate action to seize Noriega and to take him into custody only if he were offered to the United States by the rebels.[66] Unwilling to assassinate Noriega, Major Giroldi and his coconspirators released the Panamanian leader unharmed and surrendered to the forces that came to his rescue. Major Giroldi and several of his coconspirators were promptly executed, some reportedly by Noriega's own hand.[67]

As a result, the coup strengthened, rather than diminished, Noriega's stranglehold on Panama. As Secretary Baker described the aftermath:

---

[64]Baker (1995), pp. 185–186.

[65]Powell (1995), p. 419; Buckley (1991), pp. 202–203.

[66]Powell (1995), p. 419; Buckley (1991), p. 203.

[67]Buckley (1991), p. 206.

[Noriega] unleashed his intelligence operatives on the PDF, and within a matter of days they'd turned up evidence that at least two other coups were being plotted. These ringleaders, who were more senior and considerably more capable than the luckless Major Giroldi, were tortured and jailed. The end result was that contrary to public impression, the October coup strengthened Noriega's position instead of undermining it. He was now an even bigger problem than before.[68]

The one positive fallout from the coup was that it helped U.S. commanders refine their plan for the U.S. invasion of Panama that was to follow nearly three months later. American commanders went to school on the rescue of Noriega and gained vital new information about the loyalties and reaction capabilities of key PDF units. This information would lead U.S. planners to revise the targets that were to be attacked at H-hour of Operation Just Cause.[69]

The Attempts to Oust Saddam Hussein. Since the 1990 Iraqi invasion of Kuwait, U.S. leaders have sought to encourage the removal of Saddam Hussein by coup d'état. However, because they believed that the preservation of a unified Iraq was important to Gulf stability and security, U.S. decisionmakers have exhibited a marked ambivalence about attempting to promote the Iraqi leader's overthrow by popular rebellion. This ambivalence was manifest in the U.S. military and information operations conducted during the course of the Gulf War, in the U.S. refusal to militarily support the Shia and Kurd uprisings that immediately followed that conflict, and in the U.S. policy and behavior toward Iraqi opposition groups that evolved in subsequent years.

Attempts to Foment a Coup or an Uprising During the Gulf War. The planners who designed the Coalition air campaign during the Gulf War hoped that attacks on specific strategic targets might help bring down Saddam's regime in one of three ways: A direct hit might eliminate or incapacitate the Iraqi leader, or the bombing might weaken the security structure that maintained Saddam in power and spark either a coup by disaffected Iraqi military elements or an upris-

---

[68]Baker (1995), p. 187.

[69]See LTG Carl W. Stiner, Commanding General, XVIII Airborne Corps and Joint Task Force South (JCIT 024), oral history interview, Fort Bragg, N.C.: Headquarters, XVIII Airborne Corps, March 2, 7, and 27 and June 11, 1990, p. 5.

ing by the population at large.   As Coalition air component commander General Horner described it, the objective was to create an environment in Iraq "where the current leadership cannot control and provide the opportunity for new leadership to emerge."[70] However, beyond voicing such general aspirations, Coalition leaders were "vague" as to just how this change of government might come about.[71] While the air planners would have preferred that Saddam be removed prior to the start of the ground campaign—as this would probably have obviated the need for a ground assault—they anticipated that any weakening of Saddam's security structure through air attack would also increase the probability of his overthrow after the conflict had ended.[72]

Coalition air planners attached high priority to the destruction of leadership bunkers and residences, communication facilities, and command-and-control sites.   Although the primary reason for attacking such targets was to deny the Baghdad leadership the ability to direct Iraqi forces in the field, the destruction of these target sets was also deemed essential for producing a change in the Iraqi government. These facilities constituted the central nervous system of the Baghdad regime that enabled Saddam and his subordinates to govern and control Iraq and its population.[73]

To create conditions more conducive to Saddam's overthrow, Coalition aircraft attacked the Baghdad headquarters of the various agencies that protected Saddam's person and enforced his hold on power, including the headquarters of the secret police, Republican Guard, special security service, military and civilian intelligence services, Directorate of Internal Security, and Ba'ath Party.[74] Attacks were also mounted on other national command-and-control centers and VIP bunkers that were thought to house senior Iraqi officials, which pre-

---

[70]Watts et al. (1993a), p. 155.

[71]Alexander S. Cochran et al., *Gulf War Air Power Survey (GWAPS), Volume I: Planning and Command Control, Part I: Planning*, Washington, D.C.: U.S. Government Printing Office, 1993, p. 157.

[72]Hosmer (1996), p. 49.

[73]Cochran et al. (1993), p. 155.

[74]All told, Coalition planners designated some 44 leadership and 146 telecommunications and C^3 sites in Baghdad and elsewhere for destruction. U.S. Department of Defense (1992), pp. 95–96. See also Hosmer (1996), p. 50.

sumably put some of the internal security, intelligence, and military personnel who were most important to Saddam's survival in power at risk. The Coalition also tried to isolate Saddam and other senior regime leaders by attacking the key Iraqi communication facilities and nodes that allowed Iraqi leaders to communicate with one another, with Iraqi military forces and government agencies, and with domestic and foreign audiences.[75]

Coalition commanders also singled out the Iraqi Republican Guard armored and infantry divisions situated along the periphery of Kuwait for particularly heavy attack. The Republican Guard forces were considered prime targets not only because they were Iraq's best-trained and best-equipped military units but also because they were thought to be among the most important elements sustaining Saddam's continued rule.[76]   Brent Scowcroft, President Bush's National Security Adviser, described the reasoning behind the decision to target the Republican Guard "wherever we could find them":

> Since these troops were also the backbone of the regime, their destruction would further undermine Saddam's grip on power. Our Arab allies were convinced, and we began to assume, that dealing Saddam another battlefield defeat would shatter what support he had within the military, which probably would then topple him. Hitting the Republican Guard went to the heart of the problem.[77]

In addition to attempting to weaken Saddam's security structure and command and control, the Coalition mounted attacks that aimed to foment antiwar sentiment and active opposition to Saddam's continued rule among Iraq's civilian population, particularly among the residents of Baghdad. Coalition air planners sought to stimulate antiregime sentiment by (1) shutting down Iraq's electric power system to "turn the lights out in Baghdad"; (2) destroying the bridges across the Tigris River in downtown Baghdad to cut the city in half and disrupt civilian commerce; (3) destroying radio, TV, and other communication facilities to sever the regime's contact with the

---

[75]Hosmer (1996), pp. 50–51.

[76]Hosmer (1996), p. 51.

[77]George Bush and Brent Scowcroft, *A World Transformed*, New York: Alfred A. Knopf, 1998, p. 433.

population and to cause the Iraqi people to feel isolated; (4) bombing other military targets in the vicinity of Baghdad to maintain psychological pressure on Iraqi leaders and the public; and (5) destroying symbolic targets, such as the Ba'ath Party headquarters, to humiliate Saddam in the eyes of the Iraqi public.[78]

The U.S. psychological operations (PSYOP) policy and practice relating to the incitement of coups and uprisings was inconsistent and often ad hoc. Even though one of the objectives of the Gulf War PSYOP plan was to encourage the "Iraqi government, people, or military to remove their dictator," none of the leaflets dropped on Baghdad explicitly called for Saddam's overthrow.[79]   Indeed, CENTCOM never approved requests from Air Force planners for leaflet drops on Baghdad that would explicitly call for Saddam's overthrow and would thus more directly support the psychological objectives of the strategic air campaign. Air planners attributed this refusal to the CENTCOM staff's hesitancy to "encourage rebellion against Saddam's regime."   According to the air planners, "CENTCOM's rationale was a mixture of deference to perceived Saudi uneasiness about seeking democratic upheaval in the Arab world along with the notion that encouraging the collapse of an enemy government at war was somehow illegal."[80]

However, U.S. aircraft operating over northern Iraq from bases in Turkey did drop two types of leaflets that explicitly called on Iraqi military and civilian populations to revolt.[81] The message on one of these leaflets called on the population to "rise up and flood the streets and alleys for the overthrow of Saddam and his supporters." The message on a second leaflet exhorted its readers to "act against Saddam now. Saddam's fall is inevitable." The messages on both leaflets were printed on the back of replicas of Iraqi 25 dinar notes.[82]

---

[78]Hosmer (1996), pp. 53–55.

[79]Some of the leaflets dropped on Baghdad did aim to generate hostility toward Saddam by blaming him for the war and the continued bombing. Baghdad received relatively few leaflets: All told, F-16s made only two leaflet drops on the capital, disseminating fewer than one million leaflets. Hosmer (1996), p. 55.

[80]Watts et al. (1993a), p. 246.

[81]These aircraft were part of U.S. Joint Task Force Proven Force.

[82]Richard Denis Johnson, *Propaganda Materials of the Persian Gulf War*, Salt Lake City, Utah: 1995a, leaflets E10 and E11.

Calls for Kurds, Shias, and other Iraqis to rise up against Saddam were also broadcast over two "black" radio stations, the Voice of Free Iraq and Radio Free Iraq, which are said to have been located in Saudi Arabia and operated by the CIA.[83] After the Coalition ground offensive commenced on February 24, 1991, the Voice of Free Iraq, which by this time claimed to be broadcasting from Baghdad, stepped up its call for an uprising, suggesting that Saddam was preparing to flee the country:

> As you can see, [Saddam] is unjustifiably and aimlessly pushing our sons into the deadly incinerator. He will inevitably lose this battle, as he has lost all previous battles. . . . Honorable sons of Iraq, do you know that Saddam has smuggled his family out of Iraq, and has smuggled out with them the remaining funds and wealth, so that he will leave Iraq in ruins and quite empty? . . . Stage a revolution now before it's too late. . . . Hit the headquarters of the tyrant and save the homeland from destruction.[84]

Although this and other clandestine broadcasts undoubtedly reached the Shia areas of southern Iraq, it is possible that these stations lacked the power to reach Baghdad and other areas of central Iraq.[85] However, such international broadcast services as Radio Monte Carlo and the BBC, which Iraqi audiences reportedly listened to and found credible, did reach all of Iraq. While these services did not engage in PSYOP, they did report the news and may have carried President Bush's February 15 remarks urging the Iraqi people and military to "take matters into their own hands, to force Saddam Hussein the dictator to step aside and to comply with the [UN] resolutions."[86]

The Coalition attacks on strategic targets in Baghdad failed to produce the coup or popular uprising in the capital the air campaign

---

[83]Philip M. Taylor, *War and the Media: Propaganda and Persuasion in the Gulf War*, New York: Manchester University Press, 1992, pp. 27, 151–153.

[84]Quoted in Taylor (1992), p. 239.

[85]For statements about the limited range of the various U.S. PSYOP and clandestine broadcast facilities, see Gordon and Trainor (1995), p. 317, and U.S. Special Operations Command, *Psychological Operations During Desert Shield/Storm; A Post-Operational Analysis*, 2nd ed., MacDill Air Force Base, Fla.: November 5, 1993, pp. 4–9.

[86]Hosmer (1996), p. 58.

planners had hoped for. Many Iraqi leadership sites and communication facilities escaped destruction. On February 23, 1991, the eve
of the Coalition ground attack, some 70 percent of the national
telecommunications, 25 percent of the military communications,
and 30 percent of the leadership targets were still operational.[87]

While the Coalition attacks on Iraqi communication nodes degraded
the Iraqi leadership's ability to command lower echelons, the redun-
dancy built into the Iraqi communication system still allowed the
centralized command and control of internal security elements and
military forces. Similarly, while the Coalition bombing of Iraqi
broadcast facilities frequently interrupted transmission, these facilities were never permanently closed down.[88]

The bombing of headquarters did not significantly reduce the large
numbers of bodyguard, police, special security, and Republican
Guard troops guarding Saddam. In the Baghdad area alone, the special security troops committed to Saddam's protection may have
numbered as many as 25,000.[89] The bombing of headquarters or
even barracks could not disable a force of this size, particularly as
Iraqi troops typically took refuge in schools or other civilian facilities when bombing seemed imminent.

The attacks aiming to foment discontent within the Baghdad population fell short of sparking a popular uprising. Attacks on Baghdad,
which occurred mainly at night, were kept relatively light because of
humanitarian and political concerns. During the single heaviest
attack on the capital on the night of February 12–13, F-117s dropped
a total of only 34 bombs.[90] While the bombing that did occur no
doubt disrupted and frightened the people of Baghdad, it hardly
provided sufficient motivation for them to rise up and depose

---

[87]The JCS battle damage assessment for February 22–23 credited the Coalition strikes
against leadership targets with the following results: leadership sites destroyed, less
than 20 percent, and leadership sites damaged, less than 50 percent. See Watts et al.
(1999b), Figure 32, p. 289.

[88]Hosmer (1996), p. 52.

[89]In times of war, the strength of the Special Republican Guard may total some 25,000
men. The various combat and rapid reaction units of the other Baghdad-based security and intelligence services may number an additional 5,000 persons. See Sean
Boyne, "Saddam's Shield: The Role of the Special Republican Guard," *Jane's Intelligence Review*, January 1999, p. 29.

[90]Hosmer (1996), p. 54.

Saddam. Even though a majority of the population would probably have been delighted to see Saddam depart, they undoubtedly realized that any attempt by an unorganized and unarmed citizenry to oust him would likely prove futile and extremely dangerous. The regime's internal security apparatus was still intact, and Saddam had a well-known reputation for dealing decisively and ruthlessly with all his opponents.[91]

Refusal to Support Postwar Shia and Kurd Uprisings. February 28, the day of the Coalition cease-fire, saw the first of a series of major spontaneous uprisings that were soon to engulf the Shia population centers of southern Iraq and most of the Kurdish towns of northern Iraq.

Both the Shias and the Kurds had long-standing grievances against the governance they had received from Baghdad over the years and had risen in revolt before. In 1920, the Shias rose massively against British rule, which led the British to hand the reins of power to the Sunni Arabs. The British believed the Sunni Arabs to be "better partners and better suited to rule" than their Shia counterparts. In 1979–1980, encouraged by the Ayatollah Khomeini's seizure of power in Tehran, the Shias once more revolted against the secular and essentially Sunni rule of the Ba'ath Party. The Kurds had also engaged in periodic revolt, first against the British and then against various Arab regimes in Baghdad. During the early 1970s, both the United States and Iran had provided covert military assistance to a Kurd uprising so as to tie down Iraqi government forces that might otherwise have been employed in cross-border aggression. The human cost of the Kurd revolt in the 1980s was estimated at no fewer than 100,000 dead.[92]

The 1991 revolts were precipitated by evidence of Iraq's catastrophic military rout in the Kuwait Theater of Operations (KTO), when troops from the Iraqi regular army units fleeing the battlefields joined with the civilian citizenry of Basra and other towns in southern Iraq to

---

[91]Hosmer (1996), pp. 54–58.

[92]See Amatzia Baram, *Between Impediment and Advantage: Saddam's Iraq*, Washington, D.C.: United States Institute of Peace, June 1998b, pp. 3–8.

stage antigovernment demonstrations.[93]   These demonstrations quickly turned into armed rebellion as the rebels used tanks and other armored vehicles to seize government and Ba'ath Party offices as well as local security and military headquarters. Within two weeks, much of southern and northern Iraq was in rebel hands.

The paucity of communication and synchronization between the groups conducting the southern uprisings severely limited their effectiveness, as did their general lack of organization and leadership. The uprising in Basra, for example, did not have a "well-forged leadership, an integrated organization, or a political or military program."[94]   Apparently, the rebels also had no plan to move on Baghdad. Nor did the Baghdadis move to join the rebellion. Instead, they are reported to have passively "waited for the revolt to come to them." Information about the real situation at the front reached the capital's population slowly, and the delay contributed to their hesitant response. The main cause of their passivity, however, was the lack of an organized opposition structure inside the capital that could mobilize and lead an uprising.[95]

The Coalition air campaign directly influenced the uprisings by encouraging the antigovernment sentiments of the regular army forces in the KTO and by contributing importantly to their catastrophic route. In addition, the Coalition air attacks on the lines of communication between Baghdad and Basra reduced the food and other resupply to southern Iraq, creating shortages that probably intensified the alienation of the southern population and contributed to their uprisings.[96]   While the uprisings did not affect Saddam's decision to withdraw from Kuwait, they probably contributed to the alacrity with which Saddam accepted the Coalition's cease-fire terms.

---

[93]Revolts also occurred in several Sunni population centers. See Faleh Abd al-Jabbar, "Why the Uprisings Failed," *Middle East Report*, May–June 1992, pp. 2–13. Members of the U.S. 101st Airborne Division reported hearing fighting between rebel and government forces in the southern Iraqi town of Al Khidr as early as February 27. For an account of the uprising in Al Khidr, see Richard Denis Johnson, *PSYOP: The Gulf War*, 2nd ed., Salt Lake City, Utah: 1995b, pp. 57–60.

[94]al-Jabbar (1992), p. 10.

[95]al-Jabbar (1992), p. 12.

[96]Hosmer (1996), p. 60.

Many of the dissident leaders apparently expected the United States to support their uprising.[97] Despite the rebel pleas to U.S. officers for weapons and communication equipment, the United States and its Coalition partners offered no military assistance to the Shia or Kurdish rebels.

The key reason for this denial of support was the concern to preserve a unified Iraq as a buffer against Iran. As former Secretary of State James Baker put it, the United States

> did not assist the insurrections militarily, primarily out of fear of hastening the fragmentation of Iraq and plunging the region into a new cycle of instability. The Shia were quite naturally perceived as being aligned with Iran, and the Kurds, who had demanded an independent state of Kurdistan for decades, were very fragmented in their leadership and were a constant source of concern to Turkey. For these geopolitical reasons, we were wary of supporting either group. We believed it was essential that Iraq remain intact, with or without a more reasonable leadership.[98]

These concerns about promoting the Lebanonization of Iraq "were bolstered by an intense reluctance within the government to do anything that might result in the eventual reinvolvement of U.S. military forces in Iraq."[99]

These reservations toward U.S. involvement apparently also ruled out any provision of covert support to the rebels. According to Secretary Baker, several senior officials from other Coalition partners advanced proposals for such covert assistance, arguing that this was the only way to divide the Iraqi military from Saddam. If the rebels were supplied with surface-to-air and antitank missiles, they would be able to defend themselves more effectively and inflict losses on Saddam's forces. A protracted and costly insurgency might be psychologically unacceptable to the Iraqi military. As one foreign minister put it to Baker,

---

[97]See Andrew Cockburn and Patrick Cockburn, *Out of the Ashes: The Resurrection of Saddam Hussein*, New York: HarperCollins, 1999, pp. 22–25.

[98]Baker (1995), p. 439. See also Bush and Scowcroft (1998), p. 489.

[99]Baker (1995), p. 439.

The military needs to know that as long as Saddam is in power, the army will have to fight a long and costly internal war. When that realization sinks in, the military will be more willing to act against Saddam.[100]

But such arguments came to naught. The proposals for covert assistance "raised a host of thorny questions" that U.S. decisionmakers apparently were unable to resolve in the affirmative:

Could such operations be mounted successfully, given the intelligence assets that the United States and its Coalition partners could bring to bear? Would such operations just foment the fragmentation of Iraq and backfire against our desire to see stability restored in the Persian Gulf? If such an effort were tried and failed, could we count on maintaining substantial UN economic and political sanctions against Iraq?[101]

Left to their own devices, the rebellions faltered and were ruthlessly suppressed, partly by Republican Guard forces. Even though the Republican Guard divisions suffered repeated attacks during the air campaign and were the principal target of the Coalition's ground campaign, most of the Republican Guard forces managed to escape to Iraqi-controlled territory and retained sufficient capability to suppress the Shia and Kurdish uprisings.[102]

In their suppression activities, Saddam's forces made effective use of the helicopter gunships whose flight had not been prohibited in the Safwan truce agreements. General Schwarzkopf had given the Iraqis permission to use helicopters to resupply Iraqi troops around the country, but never envisioned that this "logistical courtesy from victor to vanquished" would be exploited for helicopter gunship attacks against Shia and Kurdish villages.[103]

---

[100]Baker (1995), p. 440.

[101]Baker (1995), p. 440.

[102]About half the Republican Guard armored units and most of the Republican Guard infantry units deployed in the KTO survived both the bombing and the subsequent ground fighting. See Central Intelligence Agency, OIA, *Operation Desert Storm: A Snapshot of the Battlefield*, 1A 93-10022, September 1993.

[103]See Baker (1995), pp. 439–440.

Post–Gulf War Attempts to Generate Coups and Uprisings. When—contrary to expectations—Saddam was not overthrown following the Iraqi defeat in 1991, President Bush signed a "lethal finding" that instructed the CIA to covertly create conditions that would lead to a change of regime in Iraq.[104] The policy of covertly promoting Saddam's overthrow was continued under the Clinton administration. During the period since 1991, the CIA tried a number of different plans and supported a variety of different groups in its attempts to oust the Iraqi leader. The groups receiving CIA support included Kurdish dissidents in northern Iraq, Iraqi military defectors in Jordan, Shia dissidents in southern Iraq, and a coalition of Iraqi exiles based in London.[105] None of these groups proved effective instruments for Saddam's ouster; most were torn by internal quarrels and penetrated by Iraqi government intelligence agents. Their attempts to organize coups or mount attacks against regime elements were violently repressed by Saddam's military and security forces.[106]

Two failures in particular stand out. The first occurred in March 1995, when Kurdish guerrilla forces, partly trained and armed by the CIA, mounted raids against Iraqi government positions in the northern towns of Mosul and Kirkuk. The guerrillas and the CIA-supported Iraqi National Congress (INC) leaders, who helped plan the operations, hoped that the raids would spark local insurrections, generate defections from government forces, and persuade Saddam that his army would not fight for him. The raids were part of an overall INC strategy to use the guerrilla forces of the two Kurdish factions in the north to erode Saddam's power—to "hollow out the Iraqi army by making defection to the north safe."[107] The raids, however, were to be accomplished without U.S. help. Upon learning of the planned raids, the president's NSC adviser directed that the Kurds be informed that their operation had been penetrated and hence risked

---

[104]Jim Hoagland, "How CIA's Secret War on Saddam Collapsed," *Washington Post,* June 26, 1997, p. A21.

[105]Tom Weiner, "Opponents Find That Ousting Hussein Is Easier Said Than Done," *New York Times,* November 16, 1998, p. A10.

[106]Weiner (1998), p. A10.

[107]Hoagland (1997), p. A29, and Thomas, Dickey, and Vistica (1998), p. 38.

failure. The Kurds were also told that, if they went ahead with the raids, they would do so without U.S. support or involvement.[108]

The raids also had to be accomplished with limited force. One of the two main Kurdish leaders, Massoud Barzani—who along with the rival Kurdish leader, Jalal Talabani, was on the CIA payroll—refused to allow his men to participate in the raids.[109] Without support from Barzani's or U.S. military forces, Talabani's guerrillas made little progress, and the probes were rapidly terminated.[110]

Barzani subsequently turned on his Kurdish rival and his CIA benefactors in August 1996, when he invited Saddam's tanks and troops into the north, purportedly to counter Iran's support for Talabani.[111] The Iraqi army exploited the opening provided by Barzani's defection by rounding up INC personnel, destroying the CIA base, and forcing the evacuation of American intelligence officers from northern Iraq. Some 96 Kurdish dissidents were shot on the spot, and an additional 2,000 Kurds were reportedly taken back to Iraqi intelligence headquarters, where they were reportedly interrogated and then executed.[112] More than 5,000 of the most vulnerable Kurds and other Iraqis escaped to Turkey, and some of these were resettled in the United States.

A second major CIA-backed operation collapsed in June 1996 when Saddam's security service rolled up a network of Iraqi army officers who had been attempting to foment a coup. The network was being organized and run by the Iraqi National Accord, a Jordanian-based Iraqi dissident group that was apparently deeply penetrated by

---

[108]Hoagland (1997), p. A29.

[109]Different reasons are given for Barzani's refusal to join in the raids. According to one account, it was the message from the National Security Council denying U.S. support that "split the Kurds." Another account suggests that Barzani had been squabbling with Talabani over the division of money from oil smuggling. Barzani had reason to be mistrustful of the United States. His father had led a CIA-backed revolt in the 1970s, which was "sold out and abandoned" by the Americans when the U.S. client, the Shah of Iran, sacrificed the Kurds in a separate peace deal with Baghdad. See Hoagland (1997), p. A29, and Thomas, Dickey, and Vistica (1998), pp. 43–44.

[110]By one account, the raids won over about 1,000 defectors from the government forces. See Thomas, Dickey, and Vistica (1998), p. 44.

[111]James Risen, "U.S. Welcomes Kurdish Leader Who Betrayed C.I.A. in Iraq," *New York Times*, July 25, 1998a., p. A2.

[112]Thomas, Dickey, and Vistica (1998), p. 44.

agents of Saddam's security services. More than 100 Iraqi National Accord contacts within the Iraqi military were reportedly executed when the network was taken down.[113]

Stung by these setbacks, Washington officials were reluctant during the following two years to invest resources in rebuilding the Iraqi opposition.[114] Beginning in November 1998, however, the Clinton administration began to enunciate a new policy toward Iraq, one that openly embraced the goal of ousting Saddam Hussein. As part of a "deliberate, sustained" effort to overthrow the Iraqi leader, administration leaders promised to commit resources to a "practical and effective" effort to build up potential opponents.[115] Among other measures, the new plans involved encouraging Iraq's neighbors to cooperate in efforts to oust Saddam, accelerating efforts aimed at uniting feuding Kurdish and other dissident groups into a cohesive opposition, funneling some $97 million of congressionally designated aid to Iraqi opposition groups, appointing a special U.S. convoy to work with the Iraqi opposition, and stepping up covert U.S. support for Iraqi opposition activities.[116] However, no arms were provided to the opposition groups.

Administration leaders also dangled incentives for potential Iraqi rebels at the center of power in Baghdad by promising that the United States "would work to ease economic sanctions" and "work to relieve Iraq's massive economic debts" in the event that a new government assumed power. Finally, administration leaders suggested that the United States was prepared "to use effective force if necessary" to secure its goals.[117]

---

[113]Hoagland (1997), p. A29, and Thomas, Dickey, and Vistica (1998), p. 44.

[114]James Risen, "Defining the Goal in Iraq," *New York Times*, December 23, 1998b, p. A10.

[115]Thomas W. Lippman, "Two Options for Iraq in U.S. Policy," *Washington Post*, December 24, 1998, p. 14, and John Diamond, "U.S. Focus on Ousting Saddam," *Washington Times*, December 21, 1998, p. A1.

[116]Martin Sieff, "New U.S. Game Plan to Oust Saddam Described," *Washington Times*, November 21, 1998, p. 2, and James Risen and Barbara Crossette, "Even U.S. Sees Iraq Opposition as Faint Hope," *New York Times*, November 19, 1998, p. 1.

[117]See the remarks of National Security Adviser Samuel Berger in Barton Gellman, "U.S. Committed to Change in Baghdad, Berger Says," *Washington Post*, December 9, 1998, p. 28.

Degrading Saddam's security apparatus was one of the objectives of the four-day Operation Desert Fox bombing that followed the withdrawal of UNSCOM inspectors from Iraq in December 1998. The declared objective of the bombing was to diminish Iraq's ability to develop WMD and to degrade its capabilities to threaten its neighbors. In terms of these military objectives, the Desert Fox attacks proved generally successful.

But there was also a subsidiary U.S. goal:

> to kill and demoralize the elite forces closest to the Iraqi leader and to send a message to them, and to the less-politicized Iraqi army, that the United States considers supporters of the regime targets for future attacks.

As the chairman of the JCS, General Henry H. Shelton, put it: "We know who protects the center of gravity, and so that's who we targeted."[118]

Among other targets, U.S. and U.K. aircraft struck Iraqi command-and-control centers, helicopter deployment areas, and the barracks of the Republican Guard and Special Republican Guard forces. According to General Shelton, the air strikes probably killed "several individuals" who were in the upper structure of the Iraqi leadership and possibly as many as 1,600 guard troops. While CENTCOM commander General Anthony Zinni believed that the raids had "shaken" Saddam Hussein,[119] such short-lived and limited attacks were obviously unable to degrade Saddam's security apparatus sufficiently to prompt his overthrow.

Overthrowing Saddam will be no easy matter. As the target of frequent assassination attempts and other plots, Saddam has devoted extraordinary attention and resources to his personal protection. Saddam rules Iraq through a clique of longtime Ba'ath Party associates and family members, as well as more distant relatives from his Tikriti clan. This inner circle is closely tied to Saddam's policies and,

---

[118]See Dana Priest and Bradley Graham, "Airstrikes Took a Toll on Saddam, U.S. Says," *Washington Post*, January 9, 1999, p. A14.

[119]Priest and Graham (1999).

as a consequence, to Saddam's own fate. Over the years, Saddam has purged all potential rivals and dealt harshly with any opposition.[120]

For his personal protection and for the protection of his regime, Saddam continues to rely on a large and elaborate security system consisting of personal bodyguards, a division-sized Special Republican Guard security unit, secret and other police forces, and several civilian and military intelligence services.[121] The intelligence, police, and other internal security agencies have a multitude of informants in the armed forces, in government agencies, and among the civilian population. Backing up the more immediate protection forces are other units, including the Republican Guard armored and infantry divisions, that Saddam relies on to quell attempted coups and uprisings.

The leaders and key staff members of the intelligence, internal security, and military units that protect Saddam's person and power have been carefully selected for their reliability and loyalty. Many of the key unit leaders are close relatives of Saddam, and rank-and-file members are often drawn from Saddam's al-Bu Nasir tribe or from other Sunni tribes and tribal federations that have good relations with the al-Bu Nasir.[122] Because these officers and civilian officials

---

[120]Efraim Karsh and Inari Rautsi, *Saddam Hussein*, New York: The Free Press, 1991, pp. 180–190.

[121]Among the security and intelligence elements protecting Saddam were the Special Republican Guard, Special Security Service, and Military Security Service. The Special Republican Guard (which now numbers some 14 battalions) constitutes Saddam's Praetorian Guard and is responsible for the security of Baghdad. However, several of the security and intelligence services also have brigade- or battalion-sized rapid intervention forces. See Sean Boyne, "Inside Iraq's Security Network," *Jane's Intelligence Review*, July 1997, p. 312.

[122]See Amatzia Baram, *Building Toward Crisis: Saddam Husayn's Strategy for Survival*, Washington, D.C.: The Washington Institute for Near East Policy, 1998a, pp. 20–31. Saddam also works hard to ensure the loyalty of other important Iraqi tribes, which have become a prime source of his power outside Baghdad. These tribes constitute "a combination of mercenary army, local government and loyalty club, paid and patronized for maintaining order and fealty. Favored tribes get better roads and schools, welcome bounty in a country withered by sanctions for the past decade." But patronage also can nourish a potential threat to Saddam. The greater the funding from Baghdad, the more manpower the clans can support in their militias. Thus, "the stronger the tribes become, the more the Iraqi leader has to worry that they will become a weapon for his enemies." See Stephen J. Glain, "Strong Can Backfire," *Wall Street Journal*, May 23, 2000, p. 1.

are personally beholden to Saddam for their positions and have been rewarded by the Iraqi leader for their services, they have an enormous vested interest in his survival.[123]

SUPPORT OF REBELLION TO CHANGE HOSTILE POLICY

During the Cold War, the United States provided covert support to resistance movements in an attempt to make communist aggression more expensive, to deny communist forces a lodgment in a strategic area, or to tie down hostile troops so that they could not be used elsewhere. One or more of these rationales underlay the funding, arms, and other supplies the United States provided to the Polish Freedom and Independence Movement (WIN, from the Polish) during the 1950s, the anti-Chinese resistance in Tibet during the 1950s to 1960s, the Hmong and other tribal groups fighting the communist forces in Laos from 1962 to 1973, and the Kurds battling Baghdad government forces in Iraq from 1972 to 1975.[124]

The attempt to support the Polish resistance proved a debacle, as the movement was under communist control from the outset.[125] The CIA's attempt to foster resistance in Tibet also turned out to be misguided, as the Tibetan herdsmen—encumbered by their families and animals—found it almost impossible to fight as guerrillas in the Spartan Tibetan countryside. The Americans who designed and directed the Tibetan operations underestimated Chinese capabilities and lacked "any depth of knowledge about the Tibetan people or the

---

[123]Saddam, for example, selects only politically reliable officers to command his Republican Guard units and periodically gives them cars and other expensive gifts to maintain their loyalty.

[124]These resistance movements are discussed in Rositzke (1977), pp. 169–171, 173–174; John Kenneth Knaus, *America and the Tibetan Struggle for Survival*, New York: Public Affairs, 1999; William Colby, *Lost Victory*, Chicago: Contemporary Books, 1989, pp. 197–199; and Henry Kissinger, *Years of Renewal*, New York: Simon and Schuster, 1999, pp. 576–596.

[125]American and British services conducted a substantial paramilitary effort in Poland during the early 1950s in hopes of strengthening Polish resistance forces that might sabotage and slow any Soviet military advances should war break out in Western Europe. The allies air-dropped money, military supplies, and radio equipment to elements of the Polish WIN over a two-year period. The operation was terminated when it was discovered that WIN was actually under the control of the Polish security forces, which had "deliberately provoked the British and American services to supply the 'resistance organization' with support." See Rositzke (1977), pp. 169–171.

topography of their country."[126] The resistance efforts in Laos and Iraq were crushed after the United States (along with Iran, in the case of the Kurds) had withdrawn its support. At its height, the tribal resistance in Laos tied down some 70,000 North Vietnamese troops but was able to maintain a viable defense only so long as U.S. air support was available.[127]

The United States also assisted some rebel organizations for coercive purposes, to encourage foreign decisionmakers to abandon policies and behavior considered inimical to U.S. interests and to create bargaining leverage for negotiations. Such motives underlay the covert U.S. support to antigovernment elements in Indonesia, Angola, Afghanistan, and Nicaragua.[128] With the exception of Indonesia, this coercive use of rebellion proved effective and, at least in the short run, salutary for U.S. interests. The longer-term outcome in Angola has been less than satisfactory because the National Union for the Total Independence of Angola (UNITA) is faulted for much of the continued fighting there. The longer-term evolution in Afghanistan has proved catastrophic for U.S. interests: A pariah movement—the

---

[126]According to John Knaus, the former CIA official who ran the Tibetan operation, almost none of the U.S. officials who were involved in the operation had ever been to Tibet, and none spoke Tibetan. The Tibetans were poor candidates for guerrilla operations because they were accustomed to living in large encampments with their dependents and with their herds, which in some cases consisted of as many as 30,000 animals. The resistance had to operate in an infertile countryside that could barely feed its own people much less a guerrilla force. The resistance fighters could not break up into smaller guerrilla groups—as their CIA-trained handlers kept urging them to do—because the area they inhabited did "not provide sufficient cover and sustenance for them to disperse and survive." See Knaus (1999), pp. 225–226, 233–235, 297, 332.

[127]The tribes also received some direct support from Thai artillery units. See Colby (1989), pp. 198–199.

[128]The United States also provided covert assistance to elements of the noncommunist resistance in Cambodia. By sustaining a noncommunist resistance, the United States helped promote the negotiated settlement realized in the October 1991 Paris Peace Accords, which called for the withdrawal of foreign troops from Cambodia, the cessation of external arms support, the demobilization of armed forces, and the holding of elections. However, the bulk of the military leverage that generated the need for a settlement was provided by Khmer Rouge forces supported by the People's Republic of China. The noncommunist factions (the royalist Front for a United, Neutral, Cooperative, Independent, Peaceful Cambodia and the republican Kampuchea (Khmer) People's National Liberation Front) never had sufficient military strength or martial zeal to become a crucial factor in the war. See Trevor Findlay, *Cambodia: The Legacy and Lessons of UNTAC,* Oxford, U.K.: Oxford University Press, 1995, pp. 1–3, 11.

Taliban—assumed power and provided refuge to Osama bin Laden and key elements of his terrorist network.

Support to the Colonels' Revolt in Indonesia (1957–1958)

In the summer of 1957, the CIA began to provide covert support to an antigovernment revolt by dissident Indonesian army commanders stationed in Sumatra and Sulawesi (Celebes). The avowed objective of this so-called colonels' revolt was to pressure Indonesia's then-president, Sukarno, to "desist from his drift toward communism."[129] Among other concerns, the dissident colonels opposed Sukarno's decision that Western-style democracy be abolished in Indonesia in favor of something called "guided democracy" and that representatives of the Indonesian Communist Party be brought into the Jakarta government's cabinet.[130] They were also acting because they believed that Sumatra, Sulawesi, and the other islands outside Java were paying a disproportionate share of the taxes and other costs of the wasteful, corrupt, Javanese-dominated central government and were receiving inadequate military supplies and other support in return.[131]

Eisenhower administration officials shared the rebel colonels' concerns about the growing communist strength on Java. And while neither the United States nor the rebel leaders sought the overthrow of Sukarno per se, they shared a common determination to change the makeup of his government in Jakarta. The U.S. objectives in supporting the rebels were (1) to create pressure for such a new government by encouraging cooperation among and strengthening the bargaining position of the noncommunist and anticommunist ele-

---

[129]For an account of the U.S. role in the colonels' revolt by a former CIA operative who was intimately involved in the U.S. covert operation, see Joseph Burkholder Smith, *Portrait of a Cold Warrior*, New York: G. P. Putnam's Sons, 1976, pp. 225–248. See also Audrey R. Kahin and George McT. Kahin, Subversion as Foreign Policy, Seattle: University of Washington Press, 1995.

[130]In their February 1958 ultimatum to Sukarno, the rebels demanded that the Indonesian president "resume his constitutional position and rescind his unconstitutional actions," that the incumbent Djuanda cabinet return its mandate, and that Vice President Mohammad Hatta and the Sultan of Yogyakarta be empowered to form a new cabinet, which would hold office until new general elections could be held. Kahin and Kahin (1995), p. 139.

[131]Smith (1976), p. 227.

ments on Java, and (2) to ensure a fallback position of noncommunist bastions in the Outer Islands in the event that Java was lost to the communists.[132] U.S. Secretary of State John Foster Dulles apparently sought a situation whereby the United States could plausibly withdraw its recognition of the Sukarno government and transfer it to the rebel elements on Sumatra.[133]

Despite the funds, arms, and eventual covert external air support—including B-26 bombers with U.S. and Asian contract pilots—that the CIA provided the rebel forces, the colonels' revolt was rapidly suppressed.[134] In early 1958, the dissidents committed the major blunder of declaring themselves an independent government, which energized the majority of military forces that remained loyal to the concept of a unified Indonesian state to take action against the rebels. Elements of the Indonesian navy blockaded the rebels' ports, government aircraft strafed rebel troops, and army forces sent from Java progressively reduced the rebel positions in Sumatra and, eventually, those in Sulawesi. Despite frantic pleas for continued U.S. help, the CIA found it necessary to "disengage" from the operation in May 1958, following the capture of Allen L. Pope, an American pilot whose B-26 was shot down while bombing targets near the Indonesian port of Ambon.[135] By mid-June, the rebellion was in steep decline, with rebel forces having been driven from most of the key towns they had once held. However, guerrilla opposition from rebel remnants continued for several years.

To the CIA's surprise and chagrin, many of the rebel troops put up little fight.[136] The rebel troops on Sumatra proved particularly ineffective, fleeing the battlefield whenever they heard the sound of air-

---

[132]See the unpublished retrospective account of former U.S. Ambassador Howard Jones, quoted in Kahin and Kahin (1995), p. 126.

[133]Kahin and Kahin (1995), p. 124.

[134]For an account of the air operations that supported the rebels, see Kenneth Conboy and James Morrison, *Feet to the Fire: CIA Covert Operations in Indonesia, 1957–1958*, Annapolis, Md.: Naval Institute Press, 1999, pp. 82–165.

[135]See Conboy and Morrison (1999), pp. 128–143. See also Smith (1976), p. 247.

[136]The CIA has been quite sanguine about the rebels' military prospects, envisioning even possible support for the rebellion among Javanese units. See Kahin and Kahin (1995), p. 133.

craft overhead.[137] In their postmortem of the "patchwork" operation, CIA operatives attributed the ill-advised U.S. intervention to their failure to understand the shortcomings of the Indonesians they were proposing to support. According to their assessment, the fundamental flaw was

> our eagerness to support men we didn't know enough about to start with. We hoped we would learn all we needed to know about them as we went along, but we didn't find out what they were really like until they were on the battlefield. Then it had been too late.[138]

Ironically, the rebellion and U.S. intervention intensified the leftward policy shifts the United States had hoped to prevent. The rebellion significantly strengthened Sukarno's power and hastened the destruction of parliamentary democracy in Indonesia. The anticommunist parties closely associated with the rebellion (the Masjumi and the Indonesian Socialist Party) were seriously weakened, while the Indonesian Communist Party became more powerful and respectable.[139] And despite U.S. efforts to repair its relations with the Jakarta government in the years immediately following the rebellion's collapse, Indonesia's foreign policy became increasingly radicalized and anti-Western.

Support to Noncommunist Factions in Angola (1975, 1985–1990)

To counter Soviet and Cuban attempts to help propel the procommunist faction, the Popular Movement for the Liberation of Angola (MPLA), to power in the former Portuguese colony of Angola, the United States in 1975 provided about $30 million of covert military assistance to the forces of UNITA and the National Liberation Front of Angola (FNLA), which were fighting the MPLA and Cuban troops

---

[137]The rebel troops excused their lack of military ardor on the grounds that "they would not fight their Muslim brothers." Conboy and Morrison, (1999), pp. 51, 82.

[138]Smith (1976), p. 248.

[139]The prestige and power of the Indonesian Army's chief of staff, Abdul Haris Nasution, was also increased. See Kahin and Kahin (1995), pp. 217–225.

for control of that country.[140] The U.S. objective was to achieve a stalemate between the factions on the ground and then to go public with pressure on the former Soviet Union to stop its arms supply to the MPLA.[141]

This scheme was abruptly aborted, however, on December 19, 1975, when the U.S. Senate voted to cut off all further U.S. covert and overt assistance to the noncommunist factions. The U.S. House of Representatives followed suit on January 17, 1976. While the congressional opposition was motivated by a variety of concerns, including a reluctance to see the United States side with South Africa (which had sent troops into Angola to assist UNITA and the FNLA), Congress primarily wanted to forestall the United States from becoming engaged in military action in Angola, either directly or through surrogates.[142] Following the Senate vote, South Africa chose on January 23, 1976, to temporarily disengage from the conflict. The South African withdrawal and the buildup of Cuban troops, which did most of the fighting, allowed the MPLA to secure much of the country and gain widespread recognition as the legitimate government of Angola.[143]

However, even with the help of some 30,000 to 50,000 Cuban troops, the MPLA was unable to pacify the country.[144] Drawing on strong tribal backing among the Ovimbundu peoples, UNITA leader Jonas Savimbi was able to conduct a protracted guerrilla war with South African logistical and other military support.

On August 8, 1985, the way was cleared for a renewal of covert U.S. support to UNITA when the Reagan administration secured the repeal of the congressional prohibition against U.S. aid to the noncommunist factions. Renewed American covert support, including U.S.-supplied antitank and antiaircraft missiles, proved of critical

---

[140]For a discussion of the external involvement and fighting in Angola, see Stephen T. Hosmer and Thomas W. Wolfe, *Soviet Policy and Practice Toward Third World Countries*, Lexington, Mass.: D.C. Heath and Company, 1982, pp. 79–88.

[141]Kissinger (1999), p. 808.

[142]See Hosmer (1987), p. 77.

[143]Hosmer and Wolfe (1982), p. 84.

[144]Secretary of State James Baker put the eventual number of Cuban troops in Angola at approximately 50,000. Baker (1995), p. 598.

importance to UNITA's defeat of an MPLA force in October 1987, during the largest battle of the 12-year conflict.[145]

The U.S. objective in providing this assistance was to gain leverage for negotiations to broker a withdrawal of foreign forces from Angola. This U.S. diplomatic effort proved successful in December 1988, when an accord was reached whereby Cuba agreed to pull its troops out of Angola in exchange for South Africa's agreement to withdraw its forces from Angola and neighboring Namibia, with the latter then to become an independent state. The United States assumed that the departure of the Cubans would lead to an eventual political settlement in Angola, as it would sooner or later require the MPLA regime to accept a role for UNITA in the government.[146]

However, the Soviets and the MPLA appeared to believe that with the departure of South African troops, they had a chance to crush UNITA once and for all. In December 1988, the MPLA launched a major offensive that UNITA managed to contain partly because of an emergency infusion of U.S. military aid, including shoulder-fired Stinger antiaircraft missiles.[147] The ensuing battlefield stalemate allowed the United States to negotiate a peace agreement among the parties in December 1990; the provisions included a cease-fire, a timetable for free elections, guarantees concerning UNITA's political rights, and a U.S.-Soviet agreement to terminate military aid to their respective clients. Fighting between UNITA and the MPLA resumed in December 1992, after Savimbi claimed election fraud. Despite periodic cease-fires brokered by the UN, hostilities continue.[148]

Support to the Mujaheddin in Afghanistan (1979–1992)

Following the Soviet invasion of Afghanistan in December 1979, the United States began to provide covert military aid to some of the Mujaheddin groups that were fighting both the 115,000-man Soviet occupation force and the Afghan troops that remained loyal to the communist regime in Kabul. The primary U.S. objectives in provid-

---

[145]Shultz (1993), pp. 1123–1124.

[146]Shultz (1993), p. 1128.

[147]Baker (1995), p. 599.

[148]Baker (1995), p. 600.

ing this assistance were to increase the costs to the former Soviet Union of its occupation and thereby to force an eventual Soviet withdrawal from Afghanistan.[149]

The U.S. assistance, which was funneled through Pakistan,[150] in time became extensive, involving the provision of training, logistical support, and a variety of weapons and munitions. The level of U.S. assistance stepped up sharply in March 1985 and further increased in April 1986 when the United States decided to provide shoulder-fired Stinger missiles to the Mujaheddin fighters. These weapons reduced the Soviet's ability to conduct helicopter assaults and to accurately attack Mujaheddin forces from low-flying aircraft. High-level bombing proved ineffective against the dispersed and mobile Afghan guerrilla forces.[151]

The Stingers soon began to take a heavy toll on Soviet helicopter and fixed-wing aircraft, and the "tide of the conflict shifted."[152] Because of the heavy human and materiel costs of the occupation and the growing opposition within the former Soviet Union to continued Soviet intervention, President Mikhail Gorbachev announced on February 8, 1988, that Soviet forces would start withdrawing from Afghanistan on May 15 and would be out of the country entirely within ten months.[153]

External arms support to the combatants in Afghanistan continued, however, as the United States refused to terminate its arms supply to the Mujaheddin until the Soviets ended their military support to the Kabul government. Initially, the Bush administration believed it would be unwise to cut off arms until there was a political settlement in Afghanistan, as this would have locked in a military imbalance strongly in favor of the Soviet client, Mohammad Najibullah, "and an unacceptable political status quo, setting the stage for further fighting."[154] However, the United States was unable to secure a long-term

---

[149]Shultz (1993), pp. 570, 1086, 1089.

[150]Shultz (1993), p. 1091.

[151]Shultz (1993), p. 692.

[152]Shultz (1993), p. 1087.

[153]Shultz (1993), p. 1088.

[154]See Bush and Scowcroft (1998), p. 134.

solution in Afghanistan and eventually settled for a mutual U.S.-Soviet cutoff of military aid. Partly out of a desire to resolve foreign policy problems in a way that might unlock Western aid to the former Soviet Union, Gorbachev eventually agreed to terminate Soviet arms support to Kabul by January 1, 1992.[155] The arms cutoff marked the final death knell for the Najibullah regime, which was ousted in April 1992, when Mujaheddin forces entered Kabul. Although U.S. intelligence had predicted that Najibullah would "not long survive the withdrawal of Soviet troops," the Afghan leader proved unexpectedly resilient, hanging onto power for more than three years after the last Soviet forces left the country.[156]

Support to the Contras in Nicaragua (1982–1990)

In December 1981, the Reagan administration decided to provide covert U.S. support to the Nicaraguan Contra rebels, who were ready to put military pressure on the Ortega regime in Managua and "hoped to force it at least to hold honest elections." Many of the Contra leaders no doubt also harbored the hope of eventually gathering sufficient force to oust the Sandinista regime. However, former Secretary of State George Shultz contends that by aiding the Contras the United States "was not seeking the overthrow" of the Sandinista junta. Instead, Shultz maintained that the United States was pursuing the more modest aim of putting sufficient pressure on the Managua regime to "distract it from adventures in El Salvador and to induce it to accept regionwide provisions for peace and stability."[157] Washington decisionmakers, in particular, hoped to arrest Nicaragua's growing involvement in the transshipment of Soviet bloc arms to the communist insurgents in El Salvador.[158]

---

[155]See Baker (1995), p. 528.

[156]Shultz (1993), p. 1094.

[157]Shultz (1993), p. 289. Shultz's contention that overthrow was not the objective of Contra assistance is supported by Duane Clarridge, the CIA official who directed the covert operation. While acknowledging that he knew some officials within the Reagan administration who did advocate the Sandinistas' overthrow, Clarridge holds that the charge that the United States intended to oust the Sandinista regime physically was "ridiculous," in that "we did not have the capability to do that—barring direct U.S. military involvement, which Reagan had categorically rejected from the outset." Clarridge (1997), p. 232.

[158]Shultz (1993), p. 426.

Washington officials believed that "Contra pressure and the Ortega regime's fear that the United States might try a Grenada-style operation in Managua" might give U.S. diplomatic efforts "at least some foundation in strength."[159] Through the Contradora process—the regional effort to bring peace to Central America—the United States sought an end to Sandinista support for insurgency and subversion, the removal of external-communist military advisers from Nicaragua, a reduction in Sandinista military capabilities, and the fulfillment of the Sandinistas' 1979 pledge to the Organization of American States "to govern through democratic practices."[160] In return for the Sandinistas' agreement on these four steps, the United States was prepared to end its support of the Contras and to reduce its military activities in the region.[161]

The U.S. support operations included the training, equipping, and sustaining of Contra forces in their Honduran base areas and the aerial resupply of Contra units conducting missions in Nicaragua. The United States also conducted military exercises in Honduras in an attempt to deter Sandinista attacks on that country and to reassure the Honduran government of U.S. support. These exercises may also have been intended to increase the Sandinistas' anxieties about a possible future U.S. Grenada-style takedown of their regime.

Although the Contras had no difficulty finding recruits—they rapidly built a force of some 20,000 fighters—they never acquired the equipment or numbers to take on the Sandinista army, with its thousands of troops and large stockpiles of tanks, artillery, and aircraft. In particular, the Contras lacked the capability to take the battle to the lowlands of Nicaragua, "the only locale where a denouement of the Sandinistas could be affected."[162] They even lacked the capability to control towns or to conduct sustained operations within the Nicaraguan highlands and were therefore generally limited to cross-border raiding forays. Among other targets, the Contras attacked

---

[159]Shultz (1993), p. 421.

[160]The Contradora process involved the sponsoring countries of Colombia, Mexico, Panama, and Venezuela and the so-called Central American Core Four—Costa Rica, El Salvador, Guatemala, Honduras—plus Nicaragua. See Shultz (1993), pp. 402, 951.

[161]Shultz (1993), p. 402.

[162]For a discussion of Contra recruitment and military limitations, see Clarridge (1997), pp. 231–232, 238, 243.

vehicle parks, bridges, power stations and transformer clusters, and the storage depots of the "much despised" agricultural collectives.[163]

Funding the Contra operations proved a recurring problem following the April 1984 CIA mining of Nicaraguan harbors. This act stimulated a congressional cutoff (through the passage of the third Boland Amendment) of all U.S. funds to the Contras during fiscal year 1985, which in turn prompted U.S. operatives to divert to the Contras payments made by Iran during the course of the 1986 U.S. "arms-for-hostages" weapon transfers.[164] Even though the Congress agreed to restore U.S. assistance to the Contras when it approved a Reagan administration fiscal year 1987 request for $100 million in aid, funding for military support to the rebels became increasingly difficult.[165]

Secretary Shultz believed pressure from the Contras to be critical for getting the Sandinistas to the bargaining table and to the success of the negotiating effort in Contradora. Indeed, the Ortega regime consistently sought to make progress in the negotiations contingent on the termination of U.S. support to the Contras.[166] Despite the Contras' limited military prowess and persistent funding problems, the Sandinistas apparently viewed the presence of the rebel force in Honduras as a sufficient long-term threat to warrant concessions on their part to secure Contra demobilization.

On August 7, 1987, Ortega signed Esquipulus II, a peace plan that called for a cease-fire between the Sandinistas and the Contras; a termination of U.S. support to the Contras and a cutoff of Soviet aid to the Sandinistas; and "free, pluralistic, and fair elections" in Nicaragua.[167] The implementation of Esquipulus II proved a labori-

---

[163]See Clarridge (1997), pp. 219, 232, 264.

[164]Shultz (1993), p. 839.

[165]In February 1988, Congress voted down an administration request for $36 million in aid even though only $3.6 million of that had been earmarked for military aid. Once the Contras had agreed to a cease-fire in March 1988, Congress voted them $48 million in nonlethal aid and then appropriated another $27 million to keep them in their Honduran safe havens until March 31, 1989. See Baker (1995), p. 52, and Shultz (1993), p. 953.

[166]According to Shultz: "The Nicaraguans sought to make progress contingent on the ending of U.S. aid to the Contras. While the Central American presidents found it difficult publicly to support Contra aid, privately (with the exception of Arias) they realized how important it was." See Shultz (1993), pp. 952–953, 956.

[167]Shultz (1993), p. 959, and Baker (1995), p. 52.

ous process, but the Sandinistas agreed in February 1988 to hold a presidential election within two years. In return, it was agreed that a plan would be formulated within 90 days to demobilize the Contras. The Sandinista agreement to hold free and fair elections was obviously based on a gross miscalculation of their electoral prospects. However, by the time elections were held on February 25, 1990, the Sandinistas were sufficiently boxed in by international election observers and the media that they were forced to accept the electoral defeat they suffered from Violeta Chamorro's coalition.[168]

WHY U.S. ADVERSARIES HAVE BEEN DIFFICULT TO OVERTHROW AND INTIMIDATE

The experience to date suggests that the United States will find it difficult to oust hostile leaders through the support of coups or uprisings. As noted previously, the few successes that occurred during the early 1950s were achieved against governments that lacked any significant backing from their country's military forces. Indeed, successful coups have been characterized by a dichotomy between the targeted regime and its military establishment, in which the regimes in power pursued policies that were hostile to U.S. interests, whereas significant elements of the country's military had reservations about those policies and usually retained a close relationship with the United States.[169]

While the United States has experienced greater success in using its support of resistance movements to extract concessions from hostile regimes, the movements that the United States supported have, with the notable exception of the Mujaheddin in Afghanistan, proved unable to oust incumbent regimes by force of arms. And the import of the Mujaheddin exception is undercut by the fact that the Mujaheddin takeover of Kabul came three years after the withdrawal of Soviet troops from the country.

The difficulty that the United States has encountered in promoting the ouster of hostile governments can be traced, to one degree or another, to the strengths of the incumbent regime and the weaknesses of the groups attempting to overthrow it.

---

[168]Baker (1995), pp. 59–60.

[169]David (1987), pp. 58–60.

Regime Strengths

Any government that the United States is likely to seek to remove by coup or uprising in the post–Cold War era will, by the nature of its internal organization and behavior, be a hard target to overthrow. Its leaders are likely to possess authoritarian, if not dictatorial, powers, invest heavily in their own protection, and manifest a willingness to employ unrestrained violence to maintain themselves in power. Among other practices, the leaders of such regimes are likely to

- Give priority to their personal security and the survival of their rule. Enemy leaders will tightly control access to their person and key governmental facilities and will assiduously guard information about their whereabouts and planned movements.

- Establish and maintain formidable military, police, internal security, and intelligence structures to protect their person and power, uncover plots and spies, and suppress coups and uprisings.[170] Enemy leaders will populate these intelligence, police, and security apparatuses with officers and rank and file, who for reasons of familial or tribal relationships, shared interests, or personal benefit are likely to remain loyal. Such security shields are inherently difficult to reduce by bombing.

- Eliminate or neutralize potential rivals before they can become serious threats and repress any actual or suspected opposition.

- Maintain tight control of their country's media and exploit the media to manipulate popular opinion.

---

[170]Penetrating such security barriers can prove extremely difficult. During the Vietnam War, U.S. military and CIA operatives inserted some 500 Vietnamese agents into North Vietnam in an attempt to establish spy networks. The omnipresent North Vietnamese security services caught all of these agents and ran several as double agents for years. See Richard H. Shultz, Jr., *The Secret War Against Hanoi: Kennedy and Johnson's Use of Spies, Saboteurs, and Covert Warriors in North Vietnam*, New York: HarperCollins, 1999, p. 340. For another account of the abortive U.S. operations to penetrate North Vietnam, see Kenneth Conboy and Dale Andrade, *Spies and Commandos: How America Lost the Secret War in North Vietnam*, Lawrence, Kan.: University Press of Kansas, 2000.

Opposition Weaknesses

A regime's strength is typically magnified by shortcomings in the makeup, organization, security, and combat strength of the opposition element or elements attempting to overthrow it.

- Opposition elements are often fractured and riven by personal rivalries, making it difficult to mount and sustain coordinated efforts against a government. Numerous separate factions make up the opposition in Iraq, including two Kurdish groups that have frequently been at loggerheads and a major Shia resistance organization supported by Iran that refuses to cooperate with U.S. efforts to unify the antiregime elements in that country.[171]

- The ethnic, religious, or tribal makeup of a particular opposition group often limits its ability to mobilize broad-based support within the country. Exile groups, which are frequently extremely fractious, sometimes have difficulty generating a significant following among the population that remains within the country.

- Military groups plotting coups and opposition elements planning uprisings often cannot maintain sufficient operations security to prevent infiltration by government agents, which makes them vulnerable to regime preemptive action.

- Regime security measures and the threat of premature exposure make it difficult for rebel or coup groups to accumulate the military prowess needed to prevail over well-armed regime forces on the battlefield.

The longevity of such leaders as Castro, Qaddafi, and Saddam stems in large part from the strength of their regimes and the weaknesses of the oppositions.

---

[171]The Tehran-based Supreme Council for Islamic Revolution in Iraq—an umbrella organization for several Shia Muslim groups—rejected both U.S. financial support and integration with other resistance elements. See "Iraqi Opposition Turns Down U.S. Help," *Washington Times*, January 21, 1999, p. A13.

COERCIVE AND DETERRENT EFFECTS OF DIRECT ATTACKS, COUPS, AND REBELLIONS

The Threat of Direct Attacks and Coups Has Had Little Effect

The prospect that the United States might mount a military attack on an enemy leader directly or attempt to foment and support his overthrow by a coup seems to have had little deterrent or coercive effect.

This is not to say that the direct attacks had no effect on the targeted leaders. As previously noted, Qaddafi reportedly was shaken and prone to bouts of severe paranoia after the 1986 U.S. air strikes. Similarly, the constant danger of attack from the air may have caused Saddam considerable anguish and possibly a loss of appetite. When Yevgeni Primakov met with Saddam on February 12, 1991, he was startled by the Iraqi leader's appearance: Saddam "looked gaunt, as if he had lost 30 or 40 pounds since their last meeting, four months earlier."[172]   During one visit to his "disguised" headquarters, Saddam, according to his former head of intelligence, showed signs of "deep anxiety."[173] The pressures caused by the Coalition's strategic attacks may have increased Saddam's incentive to bring a halt to the fighting and helped move him closer to agreeing to withdraw from Kuwait.[174]

However, Qaddafi, Saddam, Castro, Noriega, Aideed, and bin Laden all continued to pursue policies anathema to the United States after being targeted by such U.S. operations. None capitulated to U.S.

---

[172]Atkinson (1993), p. 283.

[173]See *Frontline* 'sinterview with General Samarrai ("The Gulf War," 1997).

[174]By mid-February 1991, the Coalition's pressures on Saddam to accede to its demands for an unconditional withdrawal from Kuwait included (1) continued air attacks on Iraqi strategic targets, which potentially threatened Saddam's personal survival; (2) devastating air attacks on Iraqi forces deployed in the KTO, which were being progressively weakened by losses of equipment and mass desertions; and (3) the impending Coalition ground offensive, which was likely to overwhelm the Iraqi defenders in the KTO. Despite these formidable pressures, Saddam in the end proved unwilling to withdraw unconditionally. He did, however, move significantly closer to accepting the Coalition's terms by agreeing to pull his troops out of Kuwait. See Hosmer (1996), pp. 62–65.

demands even after what appeared to be narrow escapes from direct U.S. attacks.[175]

Several factors seem to explain this behavior. First, the leaders apparently believed enhanced security measures would allow them to survive any future U.S. attacks on their persons or power. During the course of their rules, most had escaped previous assassination or coup attempts, mainly by indigenous foes unconnected to the United States, and thus had considerable confidence that they could handle such threats. Indeed, at one time, Qaddafi, Noriega, and Saddam were themselves successful coup plotters.

Second, these leaders apparently believed that their acquiescence in the policy changes demanded by the United States might severely undermine their credibility and authority among the key constituencies that maintained them in power. In cultures where machismo is an expected attribute of leadership, abject capitulation to the United States could place a leader at greater risk of assassination or overthrow than would be the case if he continued to defy the United States. The U.S. attempt to negotiate Noriega out of Panama was thwarted when the deal that was eventually agreed to between Noriega and the U.S. State Department was opposed by some junior officers in the PDF. These officers insisted "that Noriega remain in power, apparently fearing for their own skins should their boss depart." Noriega told a U.S. official that the junior officers had threatened a coup when presented with the deal and "accused him of selling out the PDF to the opposition."[176]

Finally, there are some leaders who may be willing to die rather than to abandon their policy. Hitler and the Japanese hard-line militarists who opposed surrender at the end of World War II are examples of leaders who refuse accommodation at any price. The prospect of death does not deter terrorists who seek martyrdom, such as those who destroyed the U.S. embassy and Marine barracks in Beirut.

---

[175]In some instances, U.S. demands for policy changes were explicit and publicly articulated, such as the demands that Saddam "withdraw from Kuwait" and "permit unfettered WMD inspections" or that Qaddafi "cease supporting terrorism and revolution." In other instances, the demands were implicit, such as the U.S. and UN requirement that Aideed accept the "marginalization" of the SNA's future role in Somalia.

[176]Shultz (1993), pp. 1077–1078.

The Threat of Rebellion Sometimes Produces Coercive Leverage

While not fruitful in the case of the colonels' revolt in Indonesia, U.S. support for rebellions and resistance movements has produced useful coercive leverage in other conflict situations.

As noted above, the covert support provided to UNITA in Angola and to the Mujaheddin in Afghanistan helped prompt agreements for the withdrawal of external communist military forces from those countries. The covert assistance the United States rendered to the Contras helped persuade the Sandinista regime in Nicaragua to terminate its arms transfers to the Salvadoran guerrillas and to hold democratic elections.

These successful U.S. operations shared several commonalities. In each instance, the United States

- backed resistance movements that were able to recruit large numbers of motivated fighters

- enjoyed access to proximate base areas from which to mount its support operations

- was able to sustain its support over a protracted period

- augmented the bargaining leverage derived from its support of the resistance movements with broader packages of economic and diplomatic sanctions and incentives aimed at encouraging enemy acquiescence

- pursued political-military objectives that fell short of seeking the military overthrow of the incumbent enemy regime.

The targeted regimes no doubt saw things differently, however, perceiving the U.S. military support to their opponents as obviously designed to secure their ouster.

Leaders Can Be Coerced by Bombing That Threatens Their Rule

The threat that continued bombing might spark a rebellion can also produce coercive leverage. Such was the case in Italy in July 1943, when the Allied bombing of railway marshaling yards and industrial targets in the suburbs of Rome helped precipitate Mussolini's removal from power and Italy's decision to seek a peace accord.[177] The bombing "caused factory workers to flee or fail to show up . . . [and] . . . provided Italian officials with clear evidence that the civilian population did not have its heart in the war."[178] The Italian army chief of staff made no move to discourage plotting against the Mussolini government by officers favoring a separate peace because he "feared that bombing, followed perhaps by fighting in Italy itself, might lead to a popular revolt, of which communists would take command."[179]

Concerns about potential public reactions to continued Allied bombing also helped speed war termination with Japan in 1945 and with the Federal Republic of Yugoslavia in 1999. One of the key reasons Emperor Hirohito decided to accept Allied peace terms in August 1945 was that he feared the hardships the Japanese people were suffering from the continued Allied bombing and blockade would eventually trigger a revolution that would destroy Japan's *kokutai* (social polity) and endanger the imperial house and throne.[180] By summer of 1945, Hirohito; his principal adviser,

---

[177]General Paolo Puntoni, who was King Victor Emmanuel's closest confidant, saw the bombing as the key catalytic event leading to Mussolini's ouster. However, other factors—including the heavy defeats Italian forces had experienced in North Africa and Sicily; Hitler's refusal to provide Mussolini with the arms aid he requested; the imminent prospect of an Allied invasion of the Italian mainland; and the fact that Italian military morale was at "rock bottom"—also influenced Italian officials to seek changes in Italy's leadership and war policies. See Ernest R. May, *"Lessons" of the Past*, New York: Oxford University Press, 1973, pp. 128–134. For another account of how Allied bombing helped bring Mussolini down and precipitated Italy's surrender, see Philip A. Smith (Maj, USAF), *Bombing to Surrender: The Contributions of Airpower to the Collapse of Italy, 1943*, Maxwell Air Force Base, Ala.: Air University Press, August 1998.

[178]May (1973), p. 128.

[179]May (1973), p. 133. This concern undoubtedly was based in part on the fact that the Allied bombing of northern Italian cities in the summer of 1943 had already caused strikes and rioting in those urban areas. Prime Minister Churchill also believed that another bombing of Rome would cause a "popular rising," which would prompt the Germans to "march in and slaughter everybody." See Winston S. Churchill, *The Second World War: Closing the Ring*, Cambridge, Mass.: Houghton Mifflin Company, 1951, pp. 44, 100.

[180]See Richard B. Franks, *Downfall: The End of the Imperial Japanese Empire*, New York: Random House, 1999, p. 345. See also Hert P. Bix, *Hirohito and the Making of Modern Japan*, New York: HarperCollins, 2000, pp. 523–524, and Butow (1954), p. 173.

Marquis Koichi Kido; and other members of the imperial court group knew that

> the people were war-weary and despondent and that popular hostility toward the military and the government was increasing rapidly, along with popular criticism of the emperor himself. More particularly, Kido and Hirohito were privy to Home Ministry reports, based on information from governors and police chiefs all over the country, revealing that people were starting to speak of the emperor as an incompetent leader who was responsible for the worsening war situation.[181]

Such trends were an ominous portent for the emperor and his court group. Indeed, according to Richard Franks,

> There is a great deal of direct and indirect evidence demonstrating that fear (perhaps exaggerated) of a domestic upheaval provided . . . the emperor with a powerful impetus to end the war. This collapse of domestic morale arose from the general trajectory of the war but became much more marked in the summer of 1945 due to blockade and the bombing.[182]

Similarly, Slobodan Milosevic's decision on June 3, 1999, to accept NATO's terms for settling the conflict over Kosovo was motivated in large part by the belief that NATO was poised to launch an "even more massive bombing" campaign if its terms were rejected.[183] Indeed, Milosevic and other senior Federal Republic of Yugoslavia officials had erroneously concluded that NATO was prepared to demolish Serbia's entire infrastructure, including its remaining bridges, telephone systems, factories, and electric power facilities.[184]

Milosevic had every reason to contemplate the prospect of such unconstrained bombing with trepidation. He realized that if there were no containment and reconstitution of the damage being

---

[181]Bix (2000), p. 523.

[182]Franks (1999), p. 345.

[183]See Milosevic Slobodan, interview, Belgrade Palma Television, trans. FBIS, EUP20001214000131, December 12, 2000.

[184]See Stephen T. Hosmer, *The Conflict Over Kosovo: Why Milosevic Decided to Settle When He Did*, MR-1351-AF, Santa Monica, Calif.: RAND, 2001, pp. 83–95.

inflicted by the bombing, the coming winter would greatly magnify the hardships of the Serbian people. The prospect of a prolonged denial of electric power was undoubtedly a particularly worrisome contingency, as it would have threatened the heating of 75 percent of Serbian homes, shut down the country's sewage services and water supply, and seriously impaired the processing, storage, and preparation of food. Milosevic had reason to doubt that the Serb public would have passively accepted such deprivation for long once the frigid Balkan winter set in. He almost certainly recognized that subjecting Serbia to further months of massive bombing risked decisively weakening his rule and that he could best survive in power by coming to terms and preserving a partially stable and functioning country.[185]

This experience suggests that occasions may arise where allied air attacks can increase an enemy leader's fear of overthrow and thereby encourage him to seek early war termination. Some enemy leaders may be paranoid about the internal threats to their regime and may overestimate the potential danger caused by U.S. air operations. As a result, air operations might at times provide greater negotiating leverage than they actually merit.

PREREQUISITES OF EFFECTIVE AIR SUPPORT TO COUPS AND REBELLIONS

Obviously, U.S. air intervention can neither negate many of the strengths that maintain a regime in power nor compensate for fundamental deficiencies of the groups seeking a regime's ouster. However, under the right conditions, U.S. air power could enhance the prospects of a successful coup or rebellion. American air strikes conducted prior to the outbreak of active armed opposition might help stimulate a coup or rebellion, particularly in conflict situations where significant elements of the enemy military and population already harbor serious doubts about the wisdom of continuing a prowar regime in power.

However, using bombing to actually foment a widespread popular uprising against an enemy government in time of war will prove dif-

---

[185]See Hosmer (2001), pp. 95–98.

ficult. Experience shows that enemy populations have failed to move against their governments even when those populations have been directly subjected to massive bombing. The German and Japanese publics that were exposed to prolonged and intensive air attacks remained largely passive throughout World War II. Similarly, the various U.S. attempts to use bombing and PSYOP to encourage the North Korean and North Vietnamese publics to pressure their leaders to accept allied peace terms failed. Humanitarian and legal considerations are likely to increasingly constrain attacks that may cause civilian casualties and other collateral damage in future conflicts, and will therefore limit the forms of pressure that U.S. air power can place on a populace to rise against its rulers.

The barriers to mounting a successful popular revolution during wartime are likely to be formidable. To overthrow their government or otherwise force war termination, dissidents must be able to

- Organize and communicate with other potential rebels. This can prove to be a formidable task when bombing is a constant threat, communications are monitored and tightly controlled, and government security services are ubiquitous and empowered to incarcerate or execute any suspected saboteurs, oppositionists, and defeatists. The *United States Strategic Bombing Survey* found, for example, that organized opposition activities in Germany during World War II

    were normally confined, by necessity, to a local scale, because any attempt to establish wider contacts and group connections exposed members to prohibitive risks. The "cell" system was commonly used, whereby only one member of a group knew of the existence of another in a different group.[186]

- Persuade large numbers of their fellow citizens to actively undermine their nation's war effort while their sons and other family members are still engaged with the enemy at the front. Mobilizing a massive antiwar movement becomes particularly difficult when the government controls virtually all information about the war and its origins and when a majority of the popula-

---

[186]U.S. Strategic Bombing Survey, *The Effects of Strategic Bombing on German Morale*, Vol. II, Washington, D.C., December 1946, in David MacIsaac, ed., *The United States Strategic Bombing Survey*, Vol. IV, New York: Garland Publishing, Inc., 1976, p. 101.

tion believes that their own country is fighting a just, defensive war (as was the case in Germany and Japan).

- Acquire military capabilities that can defeat the internal security forces that remain loyal to the government. Dissident civilians, if armed at all, are almost certain to lack crew-served and other heavier weapons. The only way they can acquire such weapons and the trained personnel to operate them is to persuade elements of the government's military and internal security forces to defect to their side.

If U.S. air strikes were sufficiently sustained and numerous, they might eventually weaken a regime's defenses against internal overthrow. More limited attacks, however, are unlikely to substantially degrade a regime's security structure. It is doubtful, for example, that the December 1998 Operation Desert Fox air attacks on Saddam's security forces or the subsequent U.S. air strikes against Iraqi air defense and communication facilities fundamentally imperiled Saddam's continued rule. While reportedly aimed at slowly "whittling down" Saddam's "power," "authority," and "nerves," such strikes were far too limited in scope and intensity to significantly erode the massive security structure that maintains Saddam in power.[187]

Direct U.S. air support may hold the greatest potential for significantly increasing the military prowess of coup and rebel forces. The prospects of U.S. air support might embolden otherwise quiescent dissident elements to move against a government; in an actual coup or rebellion, such support could either encourage some of the loyalist elements that might otherwise have come to the government's support to remain in their barracks or could persuade neutral elements that might otherwise have remained out of the fray to take up arms against the regime.[188] In these respects, the potential psycho-

---

[187]These strikes constituted only one part of a larger U.S. effort to "create the political and military conditions that would permit a successful change of the regime" in Iraq. See the statement of former Under Secretary of Defense for Policy Walter B. Slocombe in Steven Lee Myers and Tom Weiner, "Weeks of Bombing Leave Iraq's Power Structure Unshaken," *New York Times*, March 7, 1999, p. 4.

[188]It is also possible that in some coup situations an American air intervention might prove psychologically counterproductive, and cause nationalists who might otherwise have remained neutral to rally to the support of the government.

logical effects of direct U.S. air support could be significant. But it is the physical effects of such air support that could be the most telling.

Air Support to Coups

What Coup Forces Must Accomplish. To understand the potential ways in which direct U.S. air intervention might effectively support a coup, it is useful to examine what coup forces must be capable of accomplishing if they are to overthrow an entrenched regime. To be successful, coup forces typically require the following capabilities:

- First, the coup forces must possess sufficient strength, communications, and organization to seize or neutralize all key regime targets in a single operation. The coup forces must possess sufficient intelligence to identify the location and strength of key targets and how these targets might be "taken out" most efficiently. The most critical targets will likely be located in the capital city and are likely to include the senior political, military, and security officials who are most capable of rallying opposition to the coup; the military and security forces that immediately protect this senior leadership; and the principal government residencies, ministries, and command-and-control centers from which the leaders operate.

- Second, the coup forces will need to seize or disrupt the regime's operational communications (military radios, telephone exchanges, etc.) and its means of mass communication (the media), so that the various elements of potential loyalist resistance can be isolated. By disrupting the regime's communication links, the coup forces can prevent the onset of "networking" among the loyalist forces. By controlling the radio, television, and print media, the coup forces may be able to convince potential opponents and the population at large that the regime's overthrow is a fait accompli.

- Third, the coup must be conducted with sufficient surprise and speed to leave elements loyal to the regime little or no time to react. One of the greatest challenges for the coup group will be to maintain effective operational security so as to prevent preemptive counteractions from the regime's security force. Coup groups are likely to be most vulnerable to infiltration and compromise during their later organizational phases, when they seek to recruit an expanding circle of additional officers and units to their enterprise. Ideally, the coup should be executed when as many of the key human targets are as vulnerable as possible.

- Fourth, in the event that counterattacks are mounted by loyalist elements located inside or outside the capital city, the coup forces must have the means to contain and defeat such threats. The coup group would require sufficient battlefield awareness to be able to establish the makeup and routes of advance of any counterattacking forces.[189]

Tasks U.S. Air Power Might Perform Effectively . One can envision a number of tasks that U.S. air might effectively perform in support of a coup. These include

- denying the targeted regime the use of its fixed-wing or helicopter aircraft to suppress the coup

- interdicting the movement of loyalist armored and artillery forces

- reducing the military and security forces defending key regime leaders and facilities

- degrading and disrupting the regime's command, control, communications, and intelligence (C^3I)

- denying the regime's use of its radio and television media

- providing the coup group with platforms from which it could disseminate its own information to the public

- providing the coup group with intelligence about targets and military movements

- providing close air support to embattled coup forces

- moving friendly forces and key personnel to the places where they are most needed at crucial times.

---

[189]For discussions of the attributes of successful coups, see Gregor Ferguson, *Coup d'État: A Practical Manual*, Dorset, U.K.: Arms and Armor Press Limited, 1987, pp. 57–59, 83–163; Bruce W. Farcall, *The Coup: Tactics in the Seizure of Power*, Westport, Conn.: Praeger, 1994, pp. 41–143; and Edward Luttwak, *Coup d'État: A Practical Handbook*, Cambridge, Mass.: Harvard University Press, 1968, pp. 61–104, 146–162.

Prerequisites of Effective Air Support to Coups. U.S. decisionmakers are not likely to sanction air support and it is not likely to prove effective unless the United States is (1) willing to act overtly, (2) prepared to respond promptly, and (3) capable of communicating with coup leaders.

A Willingness to Act Overtly. While a few of the tasks listed above might be performed covertly, most would require an overt employment of U.S. air power. This would constitute a major departure from past U.S. practice, as U.S. military forces have not heretofore been called on to provide overt support to coups. The one minor exception to this pattern occurred during the Moises Giroldi coup in Panama, when U.S. Army units set up roadblocks to support the coup forces. Typically, U.S. support to coup groups has been handled in a clandestine manner so that the involvement of the U.S. government could be masked and, if need be, denied.

Any overt involvement of U.S. armed forces in a coup could entail political and diplomatic costs, especially if the coup were to fail. The fact that U.S. air support would be overt could make it difficult to secure agreement from neighboring governments to allow their bases and airspace to be used for such an intervention.

An Ability to Respond Promptly. Because most coups are likely to be decided within hours rather than days, the United States would have to be prepared to move promptly once one is under way. This would require obtaining prior agreement, both within the U.S. government and with the governments of the states from whose territory U.S. operations were to be mounted, on the potential actions U.S. forces might take. It would further require sufficient readiness to respond on very short notice.

A prompt response would also require the capability to judge quickly whether a coup had sufficient military and political prospects to merit U.S. military support. To determine if a coup should receive U.S. air support, decisionmakers would likely want to know whether (1) the coup group, if successful, is likely to pursue policies significantly more congenial to U.S. interests than the policies of its predecessor, (2) the coup has a reasonable chance of success, and (3) the U.S. air intervention would significantly increase the prospects of success. Decisionmakers would also want assurance that U.S. support would not violate Executive Order 12333, which prohibits U.S.

involvement in assassinations. Finally, decisionmakers would want to weigh the possible diplomatic and political costs if the United States provides support and if the coup still fails.

Such assessments are likely to be difficult, in that information about the capabilities and objectives of a coup group may be murky, particularly if U.S. officials had no foreknowledge of the coup and had not previously interacted with the coup plotters. However, if U.S. decisionmakers wait for the smoke to clear and the uncertainties to be resolved, they are likely to miss the window for decisive action.

The need for such precrisis planning and prompt decisionmaking was clear in the Bush administration's hesitant and ineffectual response to the Giroldi coup in Panama. According to Secretary of State Baker, the Bush administration had been caught unprepared by the coup and its decisionmaking had thus been "less than crisp."[190] In Secretary Baker's words:

> A prime opportunity to remove Noriega had been squandered. Our reaction had been wholly defensive. Instead of being so skeptical, we should have gone to Giroldi, demanded to know his plan in exchange for our help, assessed his scheme, and quietly assisted in its execution.[191]

The poor U.S. performance sparked considerable soul searching within the Bush administration. According to Secretary Baker, "All of us vowed never to let another such opportunity pass us by. If an opening ever presented itself again, the United States wouldn't be caught unprepared." President Bush "ordered intensive contingency planning to make sure the next chance to topple Noriega wasn't wasted." Within two weeks, several scenarios—most envisioning another coup by the PDF—had been vetted.[192] In addition, the administration's entire crisis-management process was revamped to permit more prompt and thorough coordination between agencies in times of crisis.[193]

---

[190]Baker (1995), pp. 186–187.

[191]Baker (1995), p. 186.

[192]Baker (1995), pp. 186–187.

[193]The most important of these changes was the strengthening of the role of the Deputies' Committee in moments of crisis. Baker (1995), p. 186.

A Capability to Communicate with the Coup Leaders. A third essential condition for effective air support is prompt communication and liaison with the coup leaders. American commanders will want to know the coup group's concept of operations, the identification and location of coup forces and the forces that remain loyal to the government, and the nature and exact locale of the U.S. air intervention that is most needed. To minimize fratricide, communication would need to be particularly precise and timely in the event that U.S. aircraft were asked to provide close support to hard-pressed coup forces.[194] Ideally, U.S. commanders would like to have U.S. liaison personnel on the ground with the coup leaders, but U.S. decision-makers would probably be reluctant to risk the political and diplomatic costs that could stem from the capture or death of U.S. personnel in a failed coup attempt.

Liaison and communication would be much easier were they to be preceded by coordination and joint planning between the coup leaders and U.S. commanders prior to the coup. However, this may not be feasible or desirable from the coup plotter's standpoint. Interaction with U.S. personnel might prove difficult and might increase the risks of compromise. There is more than a little truth to the adage that "when the United States knows about a coup beforehand the target government is also likely to know about the coup." Moreover, the coup forces may exploit a window of opportunity that could not be anticipated beforehand. The coup conducted in 1959 by Brigadier General Abdul Karim el Kassim against the Nuri Said government in Iraq became possible when Kassim's troops were unexpectedly permitted to move through Baghdad without first having to unload their weapons, as the government had required in previous troop movements.

Air Support to Rebellions

What Rebellions Must Accomplish. Rebellions can cover a wide spectrum of dissident activity ranging from the spontaneous, sudden popular uprisings that sometimes engulf discredited regimes to the

---

[194]Inasmuch as the fighting during coups is likely to be centered in built-up areas, the U.S. air support would have to be conducted so as to minimize civilian casualties and collateral damage.

protracted insurrections often conducted by alienated ethnic, religious, or political groups. To seize power, rebellions must accumulate—through recruitment, defection, or outside assistance—sufficient military force to defeat the military and security forces defending the government.

To oust a regime protected by numerous heavily armed military units, insurgents must be able to progressively expand their forces and move to higher levels of warfare. As Vo Nguyen Giap, the former Democratic Republic of Vietnam minister of defense, put it in reviewing the Viet Minh's successful war against the French: "The general law of a long revolutionary war is usually to go through three stages: defensive, equilibrium, and offensive." To accomplish this transition, the "guerrilla war must multiply." The "guiding principle of fighting" is to upgrade the guerrilla war "gradually to regular war, from guerrilla warfare to mobile warfare combined with partial entrenchment warfare."[195]

Even if it is unable to defeat a regime militarily, a rebellion may be able to generate sufficient pressure on a regime to cause it to make concessions favorable to the United States. Thus, there may be reasons for the United States to support a particular rebellion even if the prospects for an eventual battlefield victory by the rebels seem dim.

Tasks U.S. Air Support Might Perform Effectively. Moving a rebel force from guerrilla to mobile warfare usually requires extensive external arms, training, and logistic support. External air support could facilitate and accelerate this transition by helping to protect rebel forces in their early "defensive" phase of operations and then by providing potent firepower when the forces later move to the "equilibrium" and "offensive" phases of operations. The tasks U.S. air power could perform include the full panoply of air support provided U.S. ground forces:

- protecting rebel forces from attack by regime fixed- or rotary-wing aircraft and denying the regime aerial reconnaissance and surveillance

---

[195]See General Vo Nguyen Giap, *People's War, People's Army*, New York: Praeger, 1962, pp. 101, 103–104, 107, and Hosmer (1989), p. 75.

- preventing the movement of regime forces either by ground or by air

- destroying regime tanks, armored personnel carriers, multiple rocket launchers, and artillery when in cantonment and when forward deployed

- destroying and degrading regime C^3

- providing close air support to engaged rebel forces

- providing airlift and air resupply to rebel forces

- providing surveillance, reconnaissance, and other intelligence support to rebel units

- providing command-and-control support to rebel forces.

Prerequisites of Effective Air Support to Rebellions. As with air support to coups, there are a number of essential conditions that should obtain before U.S. air power is committed to the support of a rebellion.

The Rebellion Must Be Viable. Decisionmakers must believe that the dissident group has the inherent potential to gain power if given external air support. This judgment will rest in part on assessments of the opposition's potential to (1) develop a broad base of support among the population, (2) attract large numbers of defectors and other recruits who are willing to fight for their cause, and (3) operate effectively on the urban and rural terrain where they must eventually engage government forces. Decisionmakers must also be persuaded that a rebel victory will produce an outcome consistent with U.S. interests. It will be recalled that a persistent barrier to the U.S. support of rebellion in Iraq has been U.S. concerns about the possibility of fragmenting the country and a desire to preserve a unified Iraq as a barrier to Iranian expansionism.

The United States Must Be Willing to Operate Overtly. If U.S. air support to rebel units involved attacks on regime forces, the United States would have to willing be to operate in an overt fashion. In the past, the United States has provided only limited covert air support to rebel forces, usually with unmarked, "commercial cover" or "false flag" aircraft piloted by personnel under CIA contract.

While partly designed to stimulate antigovernment opposition and prepare the battlefield for coups and rebellions, the overt U.S. air attacks against Libya (1986) and Iraq (1991–1999) had other announced objectives that could be readily justified to international and U.S. domestic audiences. The no-fly and no-drive zones that the United States maintains in Iraq provide a form of overt U.S. air support to the antiregime Shia marsh peoples in the south and the Kurds in the north. However, the avowed aim of these U.S. interventions is humanitarian and defensive, to protect these beleaguered populations from attack by Saddam's air and armored forces.[196] The provision of overt U.S. air support to opposition groups conducting offensive operations against a sovereign government would be a different matter and would likely generate criticism and condemnation of the United States in a number of foreign capitals and international forums.

Access to Proximate Bases Would Be Needed. The United States would need access to bases in neighboring countries to conduct protracted air support operations. Proximate bases may also be needed for equipping, training, and resupplying rebel forces. American forces would need to be able to protect these bases against enemy ground and air attack. If the air intervention were overt, the United States might find it difficult to secure and maintain permission for the use of foreign bases. One of the principal reasons for keeping U.S. interventions covert and "deniable" in the past has been to satisfy the political needs of the friendly countries that were "unable to stand up to publicly disclosed involvement" in programs designed to disrupt neighboring governments.[197]

---

[196]While successful in preventing Iraqi air operations in the designated areas, the no-fly zones have not prevented Saddam from mounting devastating ground operations against his Shia and Kurdish opponents. The counterinsurgency operations that Saddam's ground forces have conducted against the Shia marsh peoples have been systematic and draconian. Many of the marshes in which the Shias have lived and gained a livelihood have been drained of water, and tens of thousands of Shias have been killed since 1991. In late 1998, Clinton administration officials suggested that U.S. air power would now be used to counter any renewal of Iraqi ground attacks against Kurdish positions in the north.

[197]As George Shultz points out, a covert involvement allows foreign political figures to privately support or acquiesce in a U.S. intervention while publicly attacking U.S. policy. See Shultz (1993), pp. 289, 1118–1119. Henry Kissinger argues that any announcement of a formal U.S. intervention in the Angolan civil war would have generated opposition from all African states, including those privately seeking U.S.

Sufficient Political Backing for a Protracted Combat Involvement Must Be Obtained. Even with U.S. air support, it may take an opposition group years to build up sufficient military strength to mount a successful overthrow. As a consequence, U.S. decisionmakers must be confident that they will be able to maintain sufficient backing from the U.S. public for a protracted involvement. Leaders of the countries providing the United States with bases must also have sufficient popular backing to maintain their support over a prolonged period.

The United States Must Be Willing to Escalate, If Need Be. The United States would need to be prepared to escalate its involvement should rebel forces become overextended and come under severe attack. Rebellions take on a dynamic of their own and are not easily controlled by outside powers. It is well to recall that the principal reason the Shah of Iran cut off covert support to the Iraqi Kurds in March 1975 was that the rebellion had provoked an Iraqi counteroffensive of such magnitude that the Kurds could no longer fend for themselves. The Iranians calculated that a continuation of the struggle would require the overt intervention of two Iranian army divisions, an annual budget of $300 million, and security guarantees from the United States to deter possible Soviet military action against Iran to aid the USSR's Iraqi ally.[198]

Achieving These Prerequisites Will Be Difficult. Satisfying the above prerequisites for the commitment of U.S. air power is likely to prove difficult. It is unclear, for example, that the Iraqi opposition will be able to develop sufficient unity, popular appeal, operations security, and military potential to pose a viable threat to Saddam's rule. Former CENTCOM commander General Anthony Zinni, for example, harbored serious doubts about the viability of the badly splintered Iraqi opposition, stating in January 1999 that he did not see an opposition group that had viability "at this point" to overthrow Saddam. He further warned against a situation in which rival opposition groups might eventually oust Saddam but at the price of creating a "disintegrated, fragmented Iraq." The Clinton administration obviously shared General Zinni's reservations because it refused to

---

involvement: "They might implore our assistance but were not prepared to avow it for fear of legitimizing a whole series of outside interventions." (Kissinger, 1999, p. 802.)

[198]See Kissinger (1999), pp. 591–596.

provide lethal assistance to any of the Iraqi opposition groups that it agreed to support.[199]

It is also not clear that the countries the United States would have to rely on for proximate bases would provide such access in the event that the Iraqi opposition matured to the point where it merited and required U.S. air support. Turkey would be reluctant to see the military strength and reach of the Kurdish opposition in Iraq greatly increased.[200] Saudi Arabian leaders—while happy to see someone other than Saddam rule Iraq—might prove even more reluctant to see their territory used for offensive air operations aimed at supporting rebel elements fighting to gain power in Iraq.[201] While privately

---

[199]In October 1998, Congress passed the Iraqi Liberation Act, which authorized some $97 million in U.S. aid to the Iraqi opposition in the form of military equipment, training, and education. Thus far, the U.S.-backed training provided to the opposition umbrella group INC has largely been limited to nonlethal activities, such as public relations, emergency medical care, and war-crime investigations. However, in March 2001, a small number of INC officers received security training for the purpose of preparing them to "protect any nonlethal presence or activities in Iraq." In September 2000, the United States signed a memorandum with the INC concerning the opposition's active involvement in the collection and dissemination of information on the situation in Iraq. As of March 2001, the George W. Bush administration was also studying (at the request of Congress) the possibility of allowing INC to distribute humanitarian goods inside Iraq. There was also speculation that funding would be provided for the INC to open an office inside northern Iraq. See Eli J. Lake, "US to Give Iraq Rebels Weapons, Security Training," United Press International, February 13, 2001; Richard Boucher, U.S. Department of State Daily Briefing, March 5, 2001; "US Holding Talks on Financial Aid to Iraqi Opposition," Agence France-Presse, March 6, 2001; Philip Shenon, "U.S. General Warns of Dangers in Trying to Topple Iraq," New York Times, January 29, 1999, p. A3; Barton Gellman, "U.S. to Start Flow of Aid to Iraqi Opposition: Exile Groups Will Get No Weapons," Washington Post, May 25, 1999, p. 10; Mark Matthews and Tom Bowman, "Toppling Hussein Poses No Easy Task," Baltimore Sun, January 13, 1999; and Steven Lee Myers, "U.S. to Aid Iraqi Opposition to Develop a Military Cadre," New York Times, October 28, 1999, p. A12.

[200]In times past, Turkey has manifested some unease about the American role in creating and sustaining a Kurdish haven in northern Iraq. The Turks say the haven has been used as a sanctuary by Kurdish guerrillas, who operate in Turkey, and provides an "unwelcome model for Turkish Kurds, who would like a self-governing enclave of their own." See Stephen Kinzer, "Turkey Reassures U.S. on Air Base," New York Times, February 13, 1999, p. A5.

[201]The Saudis have made a point of refusing to allow American warplanes based on their territory to take part in what they regard as "punitive raids" against Iraq that go beyond the purposes of the no-fly zones. They object to "any nation taking matters into its own hands, and using bombing as an instrument of diplomacy." They further assert that their restrictive policy will change only if the UN Security Council authorizes the use of force against Iraq for other purposes. See Douglas Jehl, "Saudis Admit Restricting U.S. Warplanes in Iraq," New York Times, March 22, 1999, p. A6.

agreeing for the most part with the goal of "regime change" in Iraq, such Arab countries as Egypt, Saudi Arabia, and Jordan "want to see the overthrow come from within Iraq rather than from outside."[202] In sum, a considerable change in regional attitudes and opposition capabilities would likely be required before U.S. air support to an Iraqi rebellion could become a realistic option for U.S. decision-makers.[203]

---

[202]See the statement of State Department spokesman James P. Rubin in Jane Perlez, "Albright Introduces a New Phrase to Promote Hussein's Ouster," *New York Times*, January 29, 1999, p. A3.

[203]For differing views on the likely efficacy of U.S. support for rebellion in Iraq, see Daniel Byman, Kenneth Pollack, and Gideon Rose, "The Rollback Fantasy," *Foreign Affairs*, January/February 1999, pp. 24–41, and Stephen J. Solarz, and Paul Wolfowitz, "How to Overthrow Saddam" (Letter to the Editor), *Foreign Affairs*, March/April 1999, pp. 160–161.

Chapter Four

TAKING DOWN REGIMES WITH EXTERNAL MILITARY FORCE

A final way to remove a hostile government is to overthrow it with external military force. The target country would be invaded and occupied, the old regime and its security structure would be purged, and a new government would be set in place. The ground force component of such an external invasion could be provided by troops from a neighboring country, U.S. ground forces, or a coalition of U.S. and allied forces. Whatever the makeup of the ground force contingents, U.S. air power could be called on to prepare the battlefield for the invasion and to provide support to engaged forces.

RATIONALE FOR MAINTAINING CAPABILITIES TO TAKE DOWN ENEMY REGIMES

When a Takedown May Be Mandatory

A hostile regime may damage or threaten to damage U.S. interests sufficiently to impel U.S. decisionmakers to seek its removal and replacement by external force. During World War II, U.S. forces helped bring about the takedowns of the Axis regimes in Germany, Italy, and Japan. More recently, the United States employed its armed forces to remove hostile regimes in Grenada (1983) and Panama (1989) and to force the abdication of the ruling military junta in Haiti (1994).

In the case of Grenada, the United States invaded to protect the lives of U.S. medical students and to remove a regime that was thought to be providing a base for Soviet-Cuban subversion in the Caribbean, Central America, and Africa. In Panama, the U.S. motives were to protect U.S. citizens, to restore the elected Guillermo Endara government to power, and to bring Noriega to trial in the United States, where he had been indicted for drug trafficking. The United States occupied Haiti in order to return the elected government to power and to alleviate the immediate conditions that had prompted many thousands of Haitians to seek refuge in the United States.

All these post–World War II takedowns were conducted against relatively weak opposing military and security forces, and all were accomplished rapidly with minimal U.S. loss of life. Grenada and Panama, respectively, possessed about 1,500 and 7,000 regular troops, most of whom offered little resistance. Had a forcible entry been necessary in Haiti, U.S. planners expected only limited opposition from Haiti's 7,600-man army. The armed forces of Grenada, Panama, and Haiti possessed no tanks, no artillery of any significance, and fewer than a dozen APCs apiece. The weakness of the opposition no doubt made it easier for U.S. decisionmakers to order the takedown operations.

However, one can conceive of future circumstances where U.S. decisionmakers might find it necessary to order the U.S. military to conduct or support the takedown of a country possessing sizable, well-armed military forces. The contingencies that might provoke such a response could include situations where a regime:

- Caused large numbers of U.S. and allied casualties in a conflict by employing WMD. In the event U.S. citizens were killed in a WMD attack against the U.S. homeland, there would also be a public outcry for the capture and punishment of the enemy leaders responsible.

- Mounted or abetted repeated terrorist attacks against U.S. citizens and facilities. It should be recalled that the specter of continued Libyan-sponsored terrorism once prompted U.S. officials to propose that Egypt invade Libya with U.S. logistical support.[1]

---

[1]The invasion scheme, code-named "Flower Rose," was reportedly proposed to Egypt in mid-1985 by President Reagan's deputy National Security Adviser, Vice Admiral John Poindexter, and other U.S. officials. Under the plan, the United States was to supply air cover to Egyptian transport aircraft and logistical support to the Egyptian forces. The JCS had little enthusiasm for Flower Rose because they were leery of being drawn into an operation where U.S. forces might have to come to the Egyptians' rescue. The JCS estimate was that a rescue might require as many as five U.S. divisions.

- Repeated a major act of aggression that the United States had already previously helped repulse. Should North Korea again invade South Korea or Iraq again invade Kuwait, there would be strong public pressure to remove the governments in Pyongyang and Baghdad.[2]

Advantages of Takedowns

Results May Be More Lasting. A major potential advantage of takedowns is that their results are likely to be more lasting than will be the case with attacks that only eliminate one or more of a regime's top leaders. Coups and direct attacks may bring to power leaders cut in the same mold as their predecessors and essentially beholden to the same power bases. By contrast, takedowns typically result in the elimination or fundamental reform of the military and security services that maintained the previous regime in power. They also typically involve popular elections to select new governing bodies and national leadership.

Considerations such as these led the U.S. officials in October 1989 to change the existing contingency plan for Panama so as to "include taking out the entire PDF" along with the removal of Noriega.[3] As GEN Max Thurman described the options to GEN Colin Powell, going after Noriega alone was unlikely to be sufficient as the PDF was likely to perpetuate itself in power. In Thurman's view, it was "better to take it all down."[4]

Egypt's president, Hosni Mubarak, rejected the plan in part because he did not believe the United States could "keep such a sensitive undertaking secret." See Martin and Walcott (1988), pp. 264–266.

[2]American and South Korean military commanders reportedly plan "not only to repel any possible North Korean invasion but to respond by demolishing North Korea's armed forces and capturing Pyongyang, the capital." See Richard Halloran, "S. Korea, U.S. Draft Deadly Response Plan: If North Invades, Destruction Is Goal," *Washington Times*, November 19, 1998.

[3]See Powell (1995), p. 420.

[4]See GEN Maxell Thurman, former Commander-in-Chief, U.S. Southern Command, USAWC/USAMHI Senior Officer Oral History interview transcript, Carlisle Barracks, Pa., Project No. 1992-1, 1992, p. 344. LTG Carl W. Stiner, who commanded the takedown in Panama, also believed there was "a requirement to go for the head of the snake at the same time you go for his power base: i.e., his armed forces." See Stiner (1990), p. 3.

Takedowns may also be required to ensure a fundamental and lasting change in a nation's policy. The Allies' insistence on the unconditional surrender, occupation, and reform of Germany and Japan in World War II was intended to prevent a repetition of the resurgence of militarism and aggression that followed the negotiated end to World War I. President Roosevelt saw unconditional surrender as a means to rid the German people "once and for all of Nazism and Prussian militarism and the fantastic and disastrous notion that they constitute the 'Master Race.'"[5] British Prime Minister Winston Churchill put it more broadly:

> We, the United Nations, demand from the Nazi, Fascist, and Japanese tyrannies unconditional surrender. By this we mean that their willpower to resist must be completely broken, and that they must yield themselves absolutely to our justice and mercy. It also means that we must take all those far-sighted measures which are necessary to prevent the world from being again convulsed, wrecked, and blackened by their calculated plots and ferocious aggressions.[6]

In the context of the present day, there is reason to question whether Saddam's removal from power would necessarily lead to the long-term changes in Iraqi policy the United States and its allies desired. Iraq's interest in absorbing Kuwait predates Saddam's rise to power, having become openly manifest in December 1961, when the Iraqi regime of Brigadier General Kassim threatened to annex the country.[7]

Iraq's determination to acquire WMD similarly appears to reflect more than a personal idiosyncrasy of Saddam Hussein. There is reason to believe that important elements of the Iraqi security establishment see WMD as a necessary "equalizer" to guard Iraqi national security against formidable neighbors such as Iran, Turkey, Syria,

---

[5]See Winston S. Churchill, *The Second World War: The Hinge of Fate*, Boston: Houghton Mifflin Company, 1950, p. 688. For a discussion of the background and military effects of unconditional surrender in World War II, see Anne Armstrong, *Unconditional Surrender*, New Brunswick, N.J.: Rutgers University Press, 1961, pp. 5–58, 109–167.

[6]Churchill (1950), p. 688.

[7]In December 1961, Britain dispatched naval reinforcements to the Persian Gulf to deter Kassim from carrying out his threat to annex Kuwait.

and Israel. Moreover, most of Iraq's potential opponents already possess WMD. The United States and Israel are already nuclear powers, and Iran is working hard to become one. Saddam may believe that the retention of WMD is vital to maintain the loyalty of his key military followers. This would help explain why retaining WMD has taken precedence for Saddam over having the UN Security Council's embargo lifted even though that embargo has cost Iraq more than $120 billion in oil revenues since the end of the Gulf War. Any successor to Saddam who is still beholden to the same Iraqi security establishment might be equally reluctant to give up Iraq's WMD capabilities.[8]

Takedowns May Have Greater Deterrent and Coercive Potential. For leaders of enemy states, the threat of overthrow and punishment by external military forces may have a greater deterrent and coercive effect than the threat of death or removal by other means. As previously noted, such leaders as Saddam and Qaddafi are likely to believe that they can evade direct attacks and can successfully put down coups. The prospect of an invasion and occupation by an external military power, however, may appear to these leaders to be a more serious and credible threat—so long as they believed that the external power possessed the military capability, political will, and freedom of action to take down their regimes. It should be recalled that it was the perceived threat of a possible military invasion by the United States that caused Guatemalan army leaders in 1954 to force the ouster of the Arbenz government.[9] The Gulf War, the Bosnian conflict, and the invasion of Grenada also provide examples of the deterrent and coercive potential of takedown threats.

Threat to March on Baghdad. The United States used the threat of a takedown to deter Saddam's use of WMD during the Gulf War. In a meeting with Tariq Aziz on January 9, 1991, Secretary of State Baker warned the Iraqi foreign minister:

> If the conflict involves your use of chemical or biological weapons against our forces, the American people will demand vengeance. We have the means to exact it. With regard to this part of my pre-

---

[8]For a discussion of why such weapons are important to Iraq's political and military establishments, see Baram (1998), pp. 80–83.

[9]See above, p. 53.

sentation, this is not a threat, it is a promise. If there is any use of weapons like that, our objective won't just be the liberation of Kuwait, but the elimination of the current Iraqi regime, and anyone responsible for using those weapons would be held accountable.[10]

This warning was reiterated on February 20 by an unnamed senior U.S. official who declared that Iraq's use of chemical weapons would cross a

> red line beyond which all bets are off. . . . It's a red line that would compel the Coalition to change its own objectives—adopting, for instance, a march on Baghdad to find Saddam and eliminate his regime.

Whereas the Bush administration official spoke of a war crimes trial for the Iraqi leader, an unnamed senior Arab official warned of drumhead justice: "We'll use the unimaginable short of nuclear weapons" and will go to Baghdad "to find Saddam and kill him."[11]

While warnings of a possible march on Baghdad no doubt helped stay Saddam's hand with respect to the use of WMD, the most persuasive deterrent was the Iraqi expectation that the United States would employ nuclear weapons in the event that chemical or biological weapons were used against Coalition forces. Even though they never explicitly threatened the use of nuclear weapons, American field commanders made a concerted effort to stimulate Iraqi fears about possible nuclear retaliation. Without explicitly mentioning nuclear weapons during his meeting with Aziz, Baker "purposely left the impression that the use of chemical or biological agents by Iraq could invite tactical nuclear retaliation." However, these implied threats of nuclear retaliation were a bluff in that President Bush had already decided at Camp David in December 1990 that U.S. forces would not retaliate with nuclear or chemical weapons if the Iraqis attacked with WMD. According to Secretary Baker, President Bush believed that "the best deterrent of the use of weapons of mass

---

[10]Baker (1995), p. 359.

[11]Melissa Healy, "Chemical Attack Would Escalate Allied Retaliation," *Los Angeles Times*, February 21, 1991, p. A1.

destruction by Iraq would be a threat to go after the Ba'ath regime itself."[12]

Toward the end of the Gulf War when Coalition forces entered Iraq, the possibility of a takedown greatly worried Saddam. At this point, Iraqi forces were so demoralized and weakened by the Coalition air campaign that they offered little concerted resistance to the Coalition ground offensive. According to General Wafic Al Samarrai, the former head of Iraqi military intelligence who met with Saddam after the 100-hour Coalition ground campaign was under way, the Iraqi leader became "quite desperate and frightened" at the Coalition advance, thinking "that his downfall was imminent." He asked General Samarrai whether he thought the allies would come as far as Baghdad. When Saddam subsequently learned that President Bush had called for a cease-fire, Saddam's morale rose from "zero to 100."[13] However, according to General Samarrai, Saddam—still worried about a resumption of the Coalition advance—personally ordered the Iraqi generals he sent to Safwan to negotiate the terms of the cease-fire with General Schwarzkopf and Saudi General Khaled bin Sultan to accommodate Coalition demands:

> Saddam wanted to consolidate the cease-fire in any way he could and he ordered his officers to give any information they knew about the minefields and the prisoners of war. He didn't want to give the West any excuse to resume fighting. He wanted to sign a cease-fire agreement at any price.[14]

1995 Bombing in Bosnia. The coercive potential of air operations that might weaken a hostile actor's defenses against an eventual takedown was manifest by the Bosnian Serb reaction to the NATO bombing in Bosnia-Herzegovina in September 1995. The immediate trigger for the bombing was the Bosnian Serb mortaring of a market in Sarajevo on August 28, 1995, that killed 37 people. To force Bosnian Serb leaders to pull their heavy weapons out of the Sarajevo weapons' exclusion zone and to cease firing on Bosnian Muslim positions in the capital city, the United States and other NATO allies

---

[12]See Baker (1995), p. 359, and Ed Offley, "N-Threat 'Deterred Saddam,'" *Seattle Post Intelligence*, May 17, 1991, p. 1.

[13]*Frontline* interview with General Samarrai ("The Gulf War," 1997).

[14]*Frontline* interview with General Samarrai ("The Gulf War," 1997).

launched sustained air attacks (Operation Deliberate Force) against a number of Bosnian Serb strategic targets, including command-and-control centers, air defense facilities, ammunition dumps, truck parks, and bridges.

By the time these air attacks were launched, Croat and Bosnian Muslim forces had already made considerable headway in retaking territory previously seized by the Bosnian Serbs and were advancing on other key Bosnian Serb positions. While the air attacks were in no way collusive or coordinated with these Croat and Bosnian Muslim ground offensives, they nevertheless threatened to significantly reduce Bosnian Serb combat power. The attacks aimed to erode the military capabilities that had previously made the outnumbered Bosnian Serb forces "dominant": the command-and-control network, lines of communication, and scattered ammunition dumps and vehicle parks that allowed the Bosnian Serbs to redeploy their combat forces "quickly to where they were needed."[15] As one USAF officer put it:

> Just as the Bosnian Serbs were facing their greatest military challenge on the ground, the air campaign drastically undermined their ability to command, supply, and move their forces. The combination of effects placed them in a much more immediate danger of military collapse than would have the land or air offensives separately.[16]

According to the account of U.S. negotiator Richard Holbrooke, the Bosnian Serbs were stunned by the bombing and clearly viewed it as air support to their battlefield foes. When the Croats captured the key town of Donji Vakuf, thereby opening a large area of western Bosnia to further Croat advances, Bosnian Serb President Radovan Karadzic "charged that the NATO air strikes had assisted the offensive." This charge was echoed at the various meetings Holbrooke had with the Serb leadership. The Bosnian Serb military commander, General Ratko Mladic, suddenly erupted at one point in a meet-

---

[15]See the statements of General Michael E. Ryan—then the commander of NATO southern air forces who oversaw Deliberate Force—in John A. Tirpak, "Deliberate Force," *Air Force*, Vol. 80, No. 10, October 1997.

[16]Robert C. Owen, (Col, USAF), "The Balkans Air Campaign Study: Part 2," *Airpower Journal*, No. 3, Fall 1997.

ing with Holbrooke and charged that NATO was "supporting the regular Croatian Army inside our nation."[17] Serb President Slobodan Milosevic was even more specific in another meeting, claiming that NATO aircraft were "giving close air support to the Muslims and Croats."[18]

NATO's air attacks—and the prospect that further attacks might follow—not only led the Bosnian Serb leaders to accede to NATO demands relating to Sarajevo but also encouraged them to propose a general cease-fire and to enter into the negotiating process that led to the Dayton Accords. The bombing, combined with the concurrent victories of the Croat and Bosnian Muslim ground forces, the U.S. diplomatic initiatives, and "Serbia's political pressure on its Bosnian Serb cousins," persuaded the Bosnian Serb leaders to make significant concessions.[19]

The Ripple Effects of Grenada. The potential coercive effect of takedowns has also been manifest in the reaction of enemy governments to actual U.S. takedowns. The October 1983 U.S. invasion of Grenada, which demonstrated both the United States' resolve to defend its interests and Cuba's inability to defend its clients, produced immediate policy changes in Surinam and Nicaragua. The Surinam leader, Desi Bouterse, who had appeared to be moving his country "on a forced march toward Cuban-style communism," abruptly changed course a few days after the Grenada operation. Apparently fearing that his regime might also become a target of U.S. takedown, Bouterse abruptly expelled the large Cuban contingent in Surinam and "all but broke diplomatic relations with Cuba."[20]

---

[17]See Richard Holbrooke, *To End a War*, New York: Random House, 1998, pp. 144, 150.

[18]Holbrooke (1998), p. 147.

[19]Every diplomat and senior commander interviewed in one study of Deliberate Force "believed that the air campaign distinctly affected the moral resistance of the Serb leaders and, consequently, the pace of negotiations." Holbrooke perceived that the bombing caused the Serbian diplomatic resistance to weaken rapidly, "to the verge of collapse." See Owen (1997).

[20]See Shultz (1993), pp. 393, 344. The Reagan administration had become so concerned that Surinam might evolve into the first communist state on the mainland of South America, that it actively explored different options for ousting the Bouterse regime by covert means. None of the schemes—including a CIA proposal that a force of 50 to 175 South Koreans be employed to overthrow the regime—proved practical.

Nicaragua also made immediate overtures to reduce tensions with the United States. Thomas Borge, the Sandinista interior minister, said he was certain that the United States and Nicaragua could settle their differences without much trouble and suggested that the two countries should talk as soon as possible.[21] Borge also asked U.S. ambassador Anthony Quainton to let him know if the United States ever wanted to evacuate Americans from Nicaragua, as he would facilitate their departure.[22] The Sandinistas also went out of their way to reassure the United States that they would not permit the Soviets to establish bases on Nicaraguan soil.[23]

Frank McNeil, who was a U.S. State Department Latin America specialist at the time, believed that the takedown of Grenada had "created a magnificent opportunity for a durable peace in Central America":

> Managua feared President Reagan would invade them next, and gave every appearance of being prepared to go to considerable lengths to achieve settlement.[24]

Secretary of State Shultz reported that he and the president "stewed in frustration" at the U.S. inability to produce effective counteraction against a government that was "virtually defenseless." Shultz (1993), pp. 292–297.

[21]Frank McNeil, *War and Peace in Central America*, New York: Charles Scribner's Sons, 1988, p. 175.

[22]Shultz (1993), p. 344.

[23]McNeil (1988), p. 175. William LeoGrande asserts that the U.S. invasion of Grenada caused the Sandinistas to take other unilateral steps as well:

> They asked a large number of Salvadoran revolutionary leaders who had been living in Nicaragua to leave the country, and they sent home approximately a thousand Cubans, most of them civilians. Internally, the Sandinistas eased press censorship, opened a new dialogue with the Church hierarchy, released some 300 Miskito Indians imprisoned for political reasons, and offered an amnesty to the Contras including all but their leadership. Privately, the Sandinistas communicated to Washington that they had slowed the flow of material moving through Nicaraguan territory to Salvadoran guerrillas and were seeking a reciprocal gesture from the United States.

See William M. LeoGrande, "Rollback or Containment? The United States, Nicaragua, and the Search for Peace in Central America," *International Security*, Fall 1986, pp. 102–103.

[24]McNeil goes on to report that by the time the Reagan administration got around to talks with Nicaragua in 1984, "Managua had recovered its confidence as a result of the administration fiasco in mining Nicaraguan harbors and the consequent congres-

POTENTIAL CONSTRAINTS ON CONDUCTING TAKEDOWNS

Concerns About U.S. Casualties

American decisionmakers may find it too difficult or costly to conduct a takedown of an enemy regime possessing substantial military forces. The U.S. domestic support for a takedown may be marginal; as a consequence, decisionmakers may be reluctant to commit the necessary forces and absorb the casualties that might result from such an operation. An invasion and occupation of Iraq, for example, with its 380,000-man armed forces and several thousand armored vehicles, would prove far more testing for U.S. forces than were the takedowns of Grenada, Panama, and Haiti.

Should the hostile regime possess biological weapons or, even more threatening, nuclear weapons, and an effective means of delivering them, the potential costs of a takedown could increase significantly. American decisionmakers might hesitate to back the leaders of such a regime into a corner where, facing capture and execution, they might conclude that they had nothing more to lose and order the use of the weapons.

Saddam's former head of military intelligence, General Samarrai, opined that Saddam might use WMD in a conflict if he thought he was about to die: "Perhaps he would say to himself that he will be immortalized in history textbooks."[25] Iraqi officers interrogated by officials of the UN Special Commission in Baghdad reported that Saddam had ordered the commanders of Iraq's missile batteries armed with WMD to launch their missiles in the event that communications with Baghdad were severed, as a result either of a nuclear attack or of allied ground attacks on the capital city.[26]

Proximate Bases May Not Be Available

Another factor that might discourage decisionmakers from pursuing a takedown in some contingencies would be the absence of nearby

---

sional termination of assistance to the Contras." However, McNeil still believed the Sandinistas were ready to "deal on security issues." McNeil (1988), p. 175.

[25]*Frontline* interview with General Samarrai ("The Gulf War," 1997).

[26]Baram (1998), p. 81.

bases from which to conduct and support an invasion. America's allies in the region might not see the need or justification for a take-down or might be reluctant to allow their territory to be used, because they feared WMD retaliatory attacks. As a consequence, U.S. assault forces might face unacceptably high casualties if an attempt were made to conduct an opposed landing without adequate air support and aerial preparation of the battlefield.

Concerns About Longer-Term Military, Political, and Economic Costs

Decisionmakers might also worry about longer-term costs. The Vietnam experience has made U.S. leaders leery of becoming involved in situations where U.S. forces might become bogged down in protracted guerrilla warfare. Thus, the prospect that resistance might continue against American occupation forces could help deter U.S. intervention. U.S. leaders might also be loath to accept the long-term obligations and costs of an occupying power. Here, U.S. leaders might be mindful of the manpower costs associated with the protracted U.S. occupations of Germany and Japan after World War II.[27] Finally, U.S. leaders might be concerned that international support and sanction for a takedown would be lacking.

Why U.S. Forces Did Not Go to Baghdad

It will be recalled that many of the above concerns inhibited the United States from marching on Baghdad at the end of the Gulf War.[28] One reason U.S. decisionmakers did not occupy all of Iraq

---

[27]The U.S. Army-administered military government in Germany lasted some four years, and the occupation ten years. Whereas the United States had 61 divisions and 1,622,000 men in Germany on V-E Day, the occupying force had shrunk to some 200,000 troops before the end of 1946. At its peak, the U.S. occupation force in Japan numbered around 450,000 but fell to 200,000 by February 1946. Throughout the six and one-half years of the U.S. occupation, the Army maintained an average of slightly more than 100,000 troops on duty in Japan. See Earl F. Ziemke, *The U.S. Army in the Occupation of Germany 1944–1946*, Washington, D.C.: Center of Military History, United States Army, 1990, pp. 320, 423, and John Curtis Perry, *Beneath the Eagle's Wings: Americans in Occupied Japan*, New York: Dodd, Mead, & Company, 1980, pp. 48, 168.

[28]The following discussion draws upon Stephen T. Hosmer, *Weapons of Mass Destruction and the Persian Gulf War*, Santa Monica, Calif.: RAND, MR-334-AF, 1994 pp. 22–23. Government publication, not for public release.,

and remove Saddam from power is that this would have exceeded the objectives mandated in UN Security Council Resolutions 660 and 678 to secure the Iraqi withdrawal from Kuwait and "restore international peace and security in the area."[29] But even in the unlikely event that the Security Council had sanctioned a redefined mission to occupy Iraq and capture Saddam, U.S. and other Coalition leaders might still have been reluctant to commit their forces to the pursuit of such expanded objectives.

In General Schwarzkopf's view, a move on Baghdad would have alienated the Arab people and fractured the Coalition, as none of the Arab members would have participated in such an operation. Among the Coalition partners, only the United Kingdom might have agreed to join the United States in capturing Baghdad. Had this occurred, America and Britain would have been considered occupying powers under the provisions of the Geneva and Hague conventions and would have been responsible for restoring and maintaining an Iraqi government and for providing basic services for the Iraqi people. In Schwarzkopf's view, any occupation would have proved protracted: "Had we taken all of Iraq, we would have been like the dinosaur in the tar pit—we would still be there."[30]

The commander of the United Kingdom's forces in the Gulf War, General Sir Peter de la Billiere, estimated that Coalition forces could have reached Baghdad in another 36 hours of campaigning and would probably have encountered little resistance on the way. But he also thought it would have been a mistake to have attempted to do so: By pressing on to Baghdad, the Coalition "would have achieved nothing except to create even wider problems." Coalition troops would have appeared as "foreign invaders of Iraq," and the whole of the Gulf War would have come to be seen "purely as an operation to further Western interests in the Middle East."[31]

In May 1992, Secretary of Defense Richard Cheney offered several reasons for not having gone to Baghdad. Running Saddam to

---

[29]For the relevant Security Council resolutions, see U.S. News & World Report, *Triumph Without Victory*, New York: Times Books, 1992, pp. 416, 429–430.

[30]Schwarzkopf (1992), pp. 497–498.

[31]General Sir Peter de la Billiere, *Storm Command: A Personal Account of the Gulf War*, London: HarperCollins, 1992, pp. 304–305.

ground, he said, could have taken a long time, involved large U.S. forces, cost additional American lives, and entangled the United States in Iraqi internal politics:

> Once we had rounded up Saddam, then the question is what do you do. . . . You'd have to put some kind of a government in place, and then the question comes is it going to be a Shia government or a Kurdish government. Or maybe a Sunni government, or maybe it ought to be based on the old Baathist party regime or some combination thereof. How long is that government going to be able to stay in power without U.S. military support to keep it there. . . . I would guess if we'd have gone to Baghdad I'd still have forces in Iraq today. I don't know how we would have let go of that tar baby once we grabbed hold of it.[32]

President Bush and General Brent Scowcroft not only shared these concerns but also saw a broader strategic cost to U.S. national security policy in a march on Baghdad:

> [W]e had been self-consciously trying to set a pattern for handling aggression in the post–Cold War world. Going in and occupying Iraq, thus unilaterally exceeding the United Nations' mandate, would have destroyed the precedent of the international response to oppression that we hoped to establish.[33]

American leaders saw no real need to go to Baghdad because they believed Saddam would shortly be overthrown anyway as a result of the disastrous defeat Iraq had suffered. According to Richard Haass, a former member of the Bush administration's National Security Council staff, senior officials expected surviving Iraqi troops to return home and "together with their fellow citizens, rise up against the government of Saddam Hussein."[34]

---

[32]Richard Cheney, Address to a National Press Club Luncheon, transcript, Washington, D.C., Reuters, May 20, 1992.

[33]Bush and Scowcroft (1998), p. 489.

[34]Richard N. Haass, *Intervention: The Use of American Military Force in the Post–Cold War Period*, Washington, D.C.: Carnegie Endowment for International Peace, 1994, p. 35.

PREREQUISITES OF EFFECTIVE AIR SUPPORT TO EXTERNAL OVERTHROW

A Sufficient Triggering Event

Because of the military, economic, and diplomatic costs that are likely to attend a takedown, U.S. decisionmakers will require one or more triggering events to mobilize U.S. domestic and international support for an invasion and occupation. In the event of a takedown against a state with large and well-trained military forces, whose defeat might require time and cost substantial U.S. casualties, the triggering event would also have to be of great significance: one that would be perceived by the American public as causing grave damage to vital U.S. interests.

A Takedown by a Third Country Must Serve U.S. Interests

For the United States to support a takedown of a enemy state by third-country forces, two conditions would need to be met: (1) the third country would require the will and capability (if provided U.S. air support) to invade and occupy the enemy country successfully, and (2) the United States would have to be content to see that happen. It is obvious, for example, that the United States would not consider abetting or sanctioning military attacks from Iraq's neighbors that might fragment Iraq and weaken its potential as a barrier to Iranian aggression as being in the strategic interests of the United States.

Sufficient Capability to Adequately Prepare the Battlefield

Since the minimization of friendly casualties is likely to be essential to sustaining public support for a takedown, the United States will require the capability to gain air supremacy and prepare the battlefield through aerial attack so that organized opposition to the invasion and occupation will be limited and short lived. This will require proximate bases or long-range strike capabilities and sufficient aircraft, missiles, and munitions to destroy enemy C^3, armor, artillery, and fixed defenses and to decisively erode the enemy's will to fight.[35]

---

[35]To ensure sufficient psychological damage to enemy morale, enemy troops may have to be kept under attack or the threat of attack 24 hours a day for several weeks.

To conduct sustained air operations in high-threat air-defense environments, the United States will need to maintain a robust force of penetrating bombers and other attack aircraft and a large inventory of precision-guided standoff weapons.

Robust Defenses Against Possible WMD Attacks

If a hostile regime possessed nuclear or biological weapons and the means for their effective delivery, American decisionmakers might be reluctant to attempt to pursue a takedown unless they have high confidence that U.S. forces could deter or successfully defeat attacks by these weapons. The United States will also need to be able to assure the allies providing the bases for or contributing troops to the operation that the capability exists—through a combination of preventive strikes and active and passive defenses—to deter or defeat WMD attacks against their territory and forces. Among other implications, this suggests the need for robust defenses—including near-leakproof ballistic and cruise missile defenses—against all likely delivery modes.[36]

Adequate Airlift and Air Support for Ground Forces

Finally, the United States would require the capability to provide necessary C^3I, airlift, interdiction, and close support to attacking ground forces. If third-country troops were involved, U.S. commanders and air units would need to be able to communicate and interact closely on the battlefield with such forces.

ENHANCING THE THREAT OF EXTERNAL OVERTHROW

During conflict, allied statements and military operations might be orchestrated to convince enemy leaders that their regime is likely to be ousted by U.S. or other external forces unless the leaders accede to the policy changes the United States demanded. Enemy leaders are likely to give credence to the threat of a possible external overthrow if the following apply:

The Coalition air campaign that so demoralized Iraqi troops in the KTO during the Gulf War lasted 38 days. See Hosmer (1996), pp. 141–205.

[36]Hosmer (1994), p. 36.

- Statements of war aims allow for the possible total defeat and occupation of the enemy if an acceptable settlement cannot be rapidly achieved. At a minimum, senior allied officials must avoid categorical statements denying an intention to remove an enemy government forcibly.[37]

- Allied air, ground, and naval deployments and military operations against enemy deployed forces are consistent with an ultimate objective of achieving a total military victory and occupying the enemy's homeland. At a minimum, there should be a sustained air campaign to prepare the battlefield for a later ground invasion.

- The pattern of air operations against strategic targets in the enemy's rear areas is also consistent with a possible march on the enemy's capital and a subsequent military occupation.[38]

In situations in which U.S. ground forces do not become involved in the fighting and an immediate invasion of the enemy's homeland by other friendly forces is as yet militarily infeasible, the United States might seek to destroy sufficient enemy military power to weaken its capability to defend its territory from a future invasion by one or more of its neighbors or by a rebel force. In this coercive variant, air attacks would be employed to systematically reduce the enemy's armor, artillery, and aircraft inventories, munition stockpiles, and war production and repair facilities.[39]

The aim would be to persuade the enemy government and its military leaders that the local balance of military forces was likely to turn decisively against their country unless they acceded to U.S. demands. To successfully disarm an opponent, the U.S. air attacks might have to be prolonged and intensive, and the operations would require sus-

---

[37]In some past conflicts, U.S. decisionmakers have reduced their potential leverage on an enemy regime by attempting to reassure enemy leaders about the limited and benign objectives of the U.S. military involvement. One such case was the Vietnam War, when the Johnson administration went out of its way (both publicly and privately) to assure the North Vietnamese and their Chinese and Soviet allies that the United States would not attempt to overthrow the Hanoi regime or to threaten the sovereignty or territorial integrity of North Vietnam. See Hosmer (1987), p. 28.

[38]Hosmer (1996), pp. 79–80.

[39]Hosmer (1996), p. 80.

tained U.S. domestic support. The U.S. forces would also require the sensors, surveillance and reconnaissance platforms, target processing and dynamic control measures, weapon systems, and concepts of operation that would enable them to effectively attack enemy armored and artillery forces when such forces were widely dispersed, hidden under foliage, and located in hardened bunkers or civilian settings. The potential coercive effects of the attacks would, of course, be substantially reduced if the enemy expected to receive major military resupply from an outside power.[40] It would also be necessary that the target of the attack be adjoined by one or more neighbors or rebel groups with both the incentive and potential military capability to conduct an invasion.[41]

---

[40]Hosmer (1996), p. 80.

[41]Part of the coercive strategy pursued against Serbia from April to June 1999 had a rationale similar to that suggested above. Defense Secretary William S. Cohen and General Henry H. Shelton, Chairman JCS, told Congress on April 15 that NATO could effect the removal of Serb forces from Kosovo by degrading the Serbian military to the point where a "resurgent" Kosovo Albanian movement—the Kosovo Liberation Army (KLA—or UCK, as it is known in Yugoslavia)—would have the "wherewithal" to start pushing the Serb forces out of Kosovo. General Shelton argued that the bombing could produce one of two outcomes:

> One is that Milosevic would decide that there's got to be a better way, i.e., that he would like to either start negotiating or settle with NATO; or until such time as the balance of power shifts between the uniform members of the Serbs and the KLA or UCK, that he sees his resources being diminished, his military being decimated or degraded to the point that the UCK is starting to have the wherewithal to move against him and to basically start pushing him out of Kosovo.

Secretary Cohen and General Shelton presented their views in testimony before the Senate Armed Services Committee on April 15, 1999. See Bill Gertz, "Cohen, Shelton See Victory in Kosovo Without a Treaty: Bombing Can Reduce Enemy Power to That of KLA," *Washington Times*, April 16, 1999, p. A11. NATO's attempts to "systematically" and "progressively" destroy Milosevic's military forces and thereby pressure him to come to terms proved largely unsuccessful. The Serbs were able to preserve intact the vast bulk of their ground forces by dispersing them before the NATO bombing began and by making extensive use of concealment, camouflage, and hardened underground shelters. The Serb forces in Kosovo remained far stronger than their KLA antagonists and continued to dominate the battlefield throughout the course of the conflict. See Hosmer (2001), pp. 71–82.

Chapter Five

CONCLUDING OBSERVATIONS

REMOVING ENEMY LEADERS WILL BE NEITHER EASY NOR ALWAYS BENEFICIAL

Because enemy leaders devote priority attention and large resources to the protection of their person and power, they have proved hard to kill and overthrow. Moreover, history shows that the demise of a targeted leader may not necessarily produce the change in enemy policy and behavior that the attacker desires. Even worse, an ill-considered leadership attack can produce unintended consequences that are seriously detrimental to the attacker's interests.

Over the past 50 years, the United States has had no success in removing enemy heads of state by direct attack and only very limited success in promoting the overthrow of hostile regimes by coup or rebellion. The only consistently successful way the United States has been able to remove hostile governments during the post–World War II era has been by invasion and occupation—and such takedowns have been attempted only against weakly armed opponents.

WHEN LEADERSHIP ATTACKS ARE MOST LIKELY TO BE SANCTIONED

This experience suggests that it may be unrealistic for U.S. decisionmakers to rely on direct attacks or support to coups and rebellions to dissolve enemy regimes. Even so, U.S. decisionmakers are likely to continue to turn to these instruments in future conflicts and crises given the absence of other low-cost options for removing enemy leaders and the promising benefits that might accrue should such removal operations prove successful.

Decisionmakers will be most willing to sanction operations to remove an enemy leader when (1) important U.S. interests are harmed or threatened by an enemy's policy and behavior, (2) the leader targeted for attack is considered to be the key promoter or facilitator of this harmful policy and behavior, (3) the proposed U.S. operations would not violate the U.S. prohibition against assassination or the law of armed conflict, and (4) the operation holds some promise of success and can be accomplished without unacceptable human or political cost to the United States.

Direct attacks against leaders will most likely be sanctioned when they can be said to be directed against enemy facilities that serve a military or security function and when they can be embedded in a larger military campaign in which other targets are being attacked as well. Because takedowns involve the use of large military forces, risk significant U.S. casualties, and require protracted occupations, U.S. decisionmakers will resort to overthrow by U.S. forces only when they perceive other response options to be ineffective and vital U.S. interests to be at stake.

PREREQUISITES OF THE EFFECTIVE USE OF AIR POWER IN DIRECT ATTACKS, COUPS, REBELLIONS, AND TAKEDOWNS

Because leadership attacks can be extremely counterproductive, the decisionmaker must strive to determine that the likely benefits of a proposed operation will outweigh its probable costs. Past experience with unintended consequences shows that particular attention must be paid to ensuring that the potential downside consequences of the operation are adequately explored with knowledgeable area experts.

Fixed-wing aircraft and cruise missiles have become the instruments of choice for direct attacks on enemy leaders. Since such leaders tend to move frequently to foil attacks, the success of an air strike will depend importantly on the availability of accurate, near-real-time intelligence about the leader's location or predictive intelligence on his planned movements. Special penetrating weapons will be required to effectively attack command bunkers located deep underground; accurate, low-yield munitions will be needed to strike leaders who relocate to civilian residential areas.

If circumstances permit, the intervention of U.S. air power could enhance the prospects of a coup or rebellion that might otherwise fail because antiregime forces lacked the firepower and other combat capabilities necessary to prevail on the battlefield. Aiding a coup would likely prove difficult operationally, given that the outcomes of most coups are decided within hours rather than days. Washington decisionmakers would have to be prepared to commit forces promptly, and U.S. air elements would need to be poised for immediate action. Communications would have to be rapidly established with the coup leaders to coordinate operations and avoid fratricide.

Providing combat support to a rebellion, while operationally less taxing, could prove difficult to sustain politically, given that it may take years for an opposition group to gather sufficient strength to overthrow an entrenched government. Political support would have to be sufficiently steadfast—both within the United States and among the host nations providing the U.S. with bases—to permit a protracted U.S. combat involvement. Furthermore, any extensive U.S. combat involvement would have to be overt, which would constitute a major departure from past U.S. practices and might make it difficult to secure the proximate bases needed to support U.S. air operations.

Since the minimization of U.S. casualties will be an important objective in takedowns, U.S. air elements would have to be sufficiently robust to gain air supremacy and prepare the battlefield so that any organized opposition will be limited and short lived. In addition, U.S. air elements would require the capability to provide necessary airlift, interdiction, and close support to attacking ground troops.

THE DETERRENT AND COERCIVE EFFECTS OF THREATS TO REMOVE LEADERS

The prospect that the United States might attack a leader directly or attempt to foment his overthrow by a coup d'état seems to have had little deterrent or coercive effect on enemy leaders. The leaders targeted by such U.S. operations over the years proved willing to continue to pursue policies that were anathema to the United States, no doubt partly because they believed they could successfully evade or defeat such attacks. However, there have been circumstances in which enemy leaders have found it preferable to accept allied peace terms rather than run the risk that continued allied bombing would eventually prompt popular uprisings that would topple their regimes.

While not always fruitful, U.S. arms and logistical support to rebel and resistance movements has produced useful coercive leverage for the United States in several Cold War conflict situations. In each instance, the United States sought political-military objectives that fell short of seeking the overthrow of an incumbent regime and augmented the bargaining leverage derived from its support of the resistance movements with economic and diplomatic sanctions and incentives.

For leaders of enemy states, the threat of overthrow and punishment by external military force may have a greater deterrent and coercive effect than the threat of death or removal by other means. The United States may have to increasingly rely on the threat of takedowns in confrontations with enemy regimes possessing WMD. To persuade enemies that it has the political will and military capability to conduct takedowns, the United States will need to maintain robust air, ground, and naval forces. Indeed, the potential need for such takedowns should be included among the major contingencies that size U.S. forces

BIBLIOGRAPHY

Agawa, Hiroyuki, *The Reluctant Admiral: Yamamoto and the Imperial Navy*, Tokyo: Kodansha International Ltd., 1979.

Akers, Mary Ann, "Legality of Killing Saddam Debated," *Washington Times*, February 6, 1998.

al-Jabbar, Faleh Abd, "Why the Uprisings Failed," *Middle East Report*, May–June 1992.

Alon, Hanan, *Countering Palestinian Terrorism in Israel: Toward a Policy Analysis of Countermeasures*, Santa Monica, Calif.: RAND, N-1567-FF, 1980.

Altajuri, Abubaker O., "Qaddafi: Still a Dictator," letter to the editor, *Foreign Affairs*, July/August 1999.

Ambrose, Stephen E., *Ike's Spies: Eisenhower and the Espionage Establishment*, Garden City, N.Y.: Doubleday & Company, 1981.

Arkin, William H., "Baghdad: The Urban Sanctuary in Desert Storm?" *Airpower Journal*, Spring 1997.

Armstrong, Anne, *Unconditional Surrender*, New Brunswick, N.J.: Rutgers University Press, 1961.

Atkinson, Rick, *Crusade: The Untold Story of the Persian Gulf War*, New York: Houghton Mifflin Company, 1993.

Baclagon, Uldarico S., *Philippine Campaigns*, Manila: Graphic House, 1952.

Bain, David Howard, *Sitting in Darkness: Americans in the Philippines*, New York: Penguin Books, 1984.

Baker, James A., III, *The Politics of Diplomacy*, New York: G. P. Putnam's Sons, 1995.

Baram, Amatzia, *Building Toward Crisis: Saddam Husayn's Strategy for Survival*, Washington, D.C.: The Washington Institute for Near East Policy, 1998a.

_____, *Between Impediment and Advantage: Saddam's Iraq*, Washington, D.C.: United States Institute of Peace, June 1998b.

Bix, Hert P., *Hirohito and the Making of Modern Japan*, New York: HarperCollins, 2000.

"Blow the Fuhrer from the Train and Other British Plots," *New York Times*, August 2, 1998.

Board of Inquiry on the Bay of Pigs, *Operation Zapata: The "Ultrasensitive" Report and Testimony of the Board of Inquiry on the Bay of Pigs*, Frederick, Md.: Aletheia Books, University Publications of America, Inc., 1981.

"Botched Assassination Boosts Hamas, Hurts Netanyahu-Hussein Bond," interview with Geoffrey Kemp, *Washington Times*, October 8, 1997.

Boucher, Richard, U.S. Department of State Daily Briefing, March 5, 2001.

Bowden, Mark, *Black Hawk Down*, New York: Atlantic Monthly Press, 1999.

Boyne, Sean, "Inside Iraq's Security Network," *Jane's Intelligence Review*, July 1997.

_____, "Saddam's Shield: The Role of the Special Republican Guard," *Jane's Intelligence Review*, January 1999.

Buckley, Kevin, *Panama: The Whole Story*, New York: Simon and Schuster, 1991.

Bush, George, and Brent Scowcroft, *A World Transformed*, New York: Alfred A. Knopf, 1998.

Butow, Robert J. C., *Japan's Decision to Surrender*, Stanford, Calif.: Stanford University Press, 1954.

Byman, Daniel, Kenneth Pollack, and Gideon Rose, "The Rollback Fantasy," *Foreign Affairs*, January/February 1999.

Central Intelligence Agency, Inspector General, *Survey of the Cuban Operation and Associated Documents*, Washington, D.C., February 16, 1962.

Central Intelligence Agency, OIA, *Operation Desert Storm: A Snapshot of the Battlefield*, 1A 93-10022, September 1993.

Cheney, Richard, Address to a National Press Club Luncheon, transcript, Washington, D.C., Reuters, May 20, 1992.

Churchill, Winston S., *The Second World War: The Hinge of Fate*, Boston: Houghton Mifflin Company, 1950.

_____, *The Second World War: Closing the Ring*, Cambridge, Mass.: Houghton Mifflin Company, 1951.

Clarridge, Duane R., *A Spy for All Seasons: My Life in the CIA*, New York: Scribner, 1997.

Close, Raymond, "Hard Targets: We Can't Defeat Terrorism With Bombs and Bombast," *Washington Post*, August 30, 1998.

Cochran, Alexander S., et al., *Gulf War Air Power Survey (GWAPS), Volume I: Planning and Command Control, Part I: Planning*, Washington, D.C.: U.S. Government Printing Office, 1993.

Cockburn, Andrew, and Patrick Cockburn, *Out of the Ashes: The Resurrection of Saddam Hussein*, New York: HarperCollins, 1999.

Cohen, Roger, "After the Lost Wars and the Ruined Economy, 'the Greater Slobo' Falls Silent," *New York Times*, October 6, 2000a, p. A14.

_____, "Who Really Brought Down Milosevic?" *New York Times Magazine*, November 26, 2000b, pp. 43–47, 118, 148.

Cohen, William, Statement on CNN, August 21, 1998.

Colby, William, *Lost Victory*, Chicago: Contemporary Books, 1989.

Conboy, Kenneth, and Dale Andrade, *Spies and Commandos: How America Lost the Secret War in North Vietnam*, Lawrence, Kan.: University Press of Kansas, 2000.

Conboy, Kenneth, and James Morrison, *Feet to the Fire: CIA Covert Operations in Indonesia, 1957–1958*, Annapolis, Md.: Naval Institute Press, 1999.

Cullather, Nick, *Secret History: The CIA's Classified Account of Its Operations in Guatemala 1952–1954*, Stanford, Calif.: Stanford University Press, 1999.

David, Steven R., *Third World Coups d'Etat and International Security*, Baltimore: Johns Hopkins University Press, 1987.

Davidson, Phillip B., *Vietnam at War*, Novato, Calif.: Presidio Press, 1988.

Davis, Brian L., *Qaddafi, Terrorism, and the Origins of the U.S. Attack on Libya*, New York: Praeger, 1990.

de la Billiere, General Sir Peter, *Storm Command: A Personal Account of the Gulf War*, London: HarperCollins, 1992.

Diamond, John, "U.S. Focus on Ousting Saddam," *Washington Times*, December 21, 1998.

Dobbs, Michael, "Allied Strike Denounced as 'Attempt on Milosevic,'" *Washington Post*, April 23, 1999.

Donnelly, Thomas, Margaret Roth, and Caleb Baker, *Operation Just Cause*, New York: Lexington Books, 1991.

Drysdale, John, *Whatever Happened in Somalia?* London: HAAN Associates, 1994.

Engelberg, Stephen, "C.I.A. Seeks Looser Rules on Killings During Coups," *New York Times*, October 17, 1989a.

_____, "Reagan Agreed to Prevent Noriega Death," *New York Times*, October 23, 1989b.

Faiola, Anthony, "Shining Path's Leading Light Is Captured Without a Fight," *Guardian Weekly*, July 22–28, 1999.

Farcall, Bruce W., *The Coup: Tactics in the Seizure of Power*, Westport, conn.: Praeger, 1994.

Ferguson, Gregor, *Coup d'État: A Practical Manual*, Dorset, U.K.: Arms and Armor Press Limited, 1987.

Findlay, Trevor, *Cambodia: The Legacy and Lessons of UNTAC*, Oxford, U.K.: Oxford University Press, 1995.

Flanagan, Edward M., Jr. (LTG, USA, Ret.), *Battle for Panama*, Washington, D.C.: Brassey's Inc., 1993.

"Fog of War," *Washington Post*, Q&A with Lt Gen Charles Horner, 1998. Online at http://www.washingtonpost.com/wp-srv/inatl/longterm/fogofwar/hornertext.html.

Ford, Franklin L., *Political Murder: From Tyrannicide to Terrorism*, Cambridge, Mass.: Harvard University Press, 1985.

Franks, Richard B., *Downfall: The End of the Imperial Japanese Empire*, New York: Random House, 1999.

Fulghum, David A., "Glosson: U.S. Gulf War Shortfalls Linger," *Aviation Week & Space Technology*, January 29, 1996.

Gall, Carlotta, and Thomas de Waal, *Chechnya: Calamity in the Caucasus*, New York: New York University Press, 1998.

Gasiorowski, Mark, "The 1953 Coup d'État in Iran," *International Journal of Middle East Studies*, Vol. 19, 1987.

Gelb, Leslie H., "U.S. Official Reports Contact with Qaddafi Foes," *New York Times*, April 17, 1986.

Gellman, Barton, "U.S. Committed to Change in Baghdad, Berger Says," *Washington Post*, December 9, 1998.

_____, "U.S. to Start Flow of Aid to Iraqi Opposition: Exile Groups Will Get No Weapons," *Washington Post*, May 25, 1999.

Gertz, Bill, "Cohen, Shelton See Victory in Kosovo Without a Treaty: Bombing Can Reduce Enemy Power to That of KLA," *Washington Times*, April 16, 1999.

Geyer, Georgie Anne, "Syndrome That Began in Somalia," *Washington Times*, October 3, 1998.

Giap, General Vo Nguyen, *People's War, People's Army*, New York: Praeger, 1962.

Glain, Stephen J., "Strong Can Backfire," *Wall Street Journal*, May 23, 2000.

Gleijeses, Piero, *Shattered Hope: The Guatemalan Revolution and the United States, 1944–1954*, Princeton, N.J.: Princeton University Press, 1991.

Gordon, Michael R., and Bernard B. Trainor (LtGen., USMC, Ret.), *The General's War: The Inside Story of the Conflict in the Gulf*, Boston: Little, Brown & Co., 1995.

Graham, Bradley, "Missiles Hit State TV, Residence of Milosevic," *Washington Post*, April 23, 1999.

"The Gulf War: An Oral History," *Frontline*, PBS, January 28, 1997. Transcripts online at http://www.pbs.org/wgbh/pages/frontline/gulf/oral (as of July 20, 2001).

Gwertzman, Bernard, "Shultz Expresses Hopes for a Coup to Oust Qaddafi," *New York Times*, April 18, 1986.

Haass, Richard N., *Intervention: The Use of American Military Force in the Post–Cold War Period*, Washington, D.C.: Carnegie Endowment for International Peace, 1994.

Hacaoglu, Selcan, "PKK Leader Pleads for His Life," *Washington Times*, June 1, 1999.

Halloran, Richard, "S. Korea, U.S. Draft Deadly Response Plan: If North Invades, Destruction Is Goal," *Washington Times*, November 19, 1998.

Havens, Murray Clark, Carl Leiden, and Karl M. Schmitt, *The Politics of Assassination*, Englewood Cliffs, N.J.: Prentice-Hall, Inc., 1970.

Healy, Melissa, "Chemical Attack Would Escalate Allied Retaliation," *Los Angeles Times*, February 21, 1991.

Hirsch, John L., and Robert B. Oakley, *Somalia and Operation Restore Hope*, Washington, D.C.: United States Institute of Peace Press, 1995.

Hoagland, Jim, "How CIA's Secret War on Saddam Collapsed," *Washington Post,* June 26, 1997.

Hoge, Warren, "Britain Reveals Elaborate Plots to Kill Hitler as War Neared End," *New York Times,* July 24, 1998.

Holbrooke, Richard, *To End a War,* New York: Random House, 1998.

Horne, Alistair, *A Savage War of Peace: Algeria 1954–1962,* New York: Viking Press, 1977.

Hosmer, Stephen T., *Constraints on U.S. Strategy in Third World Conflicts,* New York: Crane Russak & Company, 1987.

_____, *Weapons of Mass Destruction and the Persian Gulf War,* Santa Monica, Calif.: RAND, MR-334-AF, 1994. Government publication, not for public release.

_____, *Psychological Effects of U.S. Air Operations in Four Wars 1941–1991: Lessons for U.S. Commanders,* Santa Monica, Calif.: RAND, MR-576-AF, 1996.

_____, *The Conflict Over Kosovo: Why Milosevic Decided to Settle When He Did,* MR-1351-AF, Santa Monica, Calif.: RAND, 2001.

Hosmer, Stephen T., and Thomas W. Wolfe, *Soviet Policy and Practice Toward Third World Countries,* Lexington, Mass.: D.C. Heath and Company, 1982.

Ibrahim, Youssef M., "Jordan Is Angered by Israeli Findings on Assassination Fiasco," *New York Times,* February 18, 1998.

Ignatieff, Michael, "The Virtual Commander: How NATO Invented a New Kind of War," *New Yorker,* August 2, 1999.

Immerman, Richard H., *The CIA in Guatemala: The Foreign Policy of Intervention,* Austin, Tex.: University of Texas Press, 1997.

"Iraqi Opposition Turns Down U.S. Help," *Washington Times,* January 21, 1999, p. A13.

Jehl, Douglas, "Saudis Admit Restricting U.S. Warplanes in Iraq," *New York Times,* March 22, 1999.

Jennings, Peter, "Unfinished Business: The CIA and Saddam Hussein," report, ABC News, June 26, 1997.

Johnson, Richard Denis, *Propaganda Materials of the Persian Gulf War*, Salt Lake City, Utah: 1995a.

_____, *PSYOP: The Gulf War*, 2nd ed., Salt Lake City, Utah: 1995b.

Kahin, Audrey R., and George McT. Kahin, *Subversion as Foreign Policy*, Seattle: University of Washington Press, 1995.

Karsh, Efraim, and Inari Rautsi, *Saddam Hussein*, New York: The Free Press, 1991.

Keaney, Thomas A., and Eliot A. Cohen, *Gulf War Air Power Survey: Summary Report*, Washington, D.C.: U.S. Government Printing Office, 1993.

Kinzer, Stephen, "Turkey Reassures U.S. on Air Base," *New York Times*, February 13, 1999.

Kissinger, Henry, *Years of Renewal*, New York: Simon and Schuster, 1999.

Knaus, John Kenneth, *America and the Tibetan Struggle for Survival*, New York: Public Affairs, 1999.

Koring, Paul, "Mossad Again Finds Itself in Public Glare: Amman Fiasco Recalls '73 Incident," *Washington Times*, October 8, 1997.

Lake, Eli J., "US to Give Iraq Rebels Weapons, Security Training," United Press International, February 13, 2001.

Larson, Eric V., *Casualties and Consensus*, Santa Monica, Calif.: RAND, MR-726-RC, 1996.

LeoGrande, William M., "Rollback or Containment? The United States, Nicaragua, and the Search for Peace in Central America," *International Security*, Fall 1986.

Lewy, Guenter, *America in Vietnam*, New York: Oxford University Press, 1978.

"Libya, Mystery of the Vanishing Oil Money," *Economist*, February 7, 1998.

Lippman, Thomas W., "Two Options for Iraq in U.S. Policy," *Washington Post*, December 24, 1998.

Lorch, Donatella, "U.N. Says It Will Press Effort to Disarm Somalis," *New York Times*, July 14, 1993a.

_____, "U.N. Finds Peace Elusive with Somali Leader at Large," *New York Times*, July 15, 1993b.

Luttwak, Edward, *Coup d'Etat: A Practical Handbook*, Cambridge, Mass.: Harvard University Press, 1968.

Maren, Michael, "Somalia: Whose Failure?" *Current History*, May 1996.

Martin, David C., and John Walcott, *Best Laid Plans: The Inside Story of America's War Against Terrorism*, New York: Harper & Row, 1988.

Matthews, Mark, and Tom Bowman, "Toppling Hussein Poses No Easy Task," *Baltimore Sun*, January 13, 1999.

May, Ernest R., *"Lessons" of the Past*, New York: Oxford University Press, 1973.

McConnell, Malcolm, *Just Cause*, New York: St. Martin's Press, 1991.

McFadden, Robert D., "Hussein Hints Use of All His Weapons," *New York Times*, January 29, 1991.

McNeil, Donald G., Jr., "Libyan Convicted by Scottish Court in '88 Pan Am Blast," *New York Times*, January 1, 2001.

McNeil, Frank, *War and Peace in Central America*, New York: Charles Scribner's Sons, 1988.

Melman, Yossi, "Israel's Darkest Secrets," *New York Times*, March 25, 1998.

Myers, Steven Lee, "U.S. to Aid Iraqi Opposition to Develop a Military Cadre," *New York Times*, October 28, 1999.

Myers, Steven Lee, and Tom Weiner, "Weeks of Bombing Leave Iraq's Power Structure Unshaken," *New York Times*, March 7, 1999.

Milosevic, Slobodan, interview, Belgrade Palma Television, trans. FBIS, FBIS EUP20001214000131, December 12, 2000.

O'Brien, William V., *The Conduct of Just and Limited War*, New York: Praeger, 1981.

Offley, Ed, "N-Threat 'Deterred Saddam,'" *Seattle Post Intelligence*, May 17, 1991.

Stiner, LTG Carl W., Commanding General, XVIII Airborne Corps and Joint Task Force South (JCIT 024), oral history interview, Fort Bragg, N.C.: Headquarters, XVIII Airborne Corps, March 2, 7, and 27 and June 11, 1990.

Owen, Robert C. (Col, USAF), "The Balkans Air Campaign Study: Part 2," *Airpower Journal*, No. 3, Fall 1997.

Palmer, General Bruce, Jr., *The 25-Year War: America's Military Role in Vietnam*, Lexington, Ky.: The University Press of Kentucky, 1984.

Parks, W. Hays, "Memorandum of Law: Executive Order 12333 and Assassination," *Army Lawyer*, December 1989.

Perlez, Jane, "Albright Introduces a New Phrase to Promote Hussein's Ouster," *New York Times*, January 29, 1999.

_____, "Unpersuaded by Verdict, Bush Backs Sanctions," *New York Times*, February 1, 2001.

Perry, John Curtis, *Beneath the Eagle's Wings: Americans in Occupied Japan*, New York: Dodd, Mead, & Company, 1980.

Peterson, Scott, *Me Against My Brother*, New York: Routledge, 2000.

Powell, Colin, *My American Journey*, New York: Random House, 1995.

Prados, John, *Presidents' Secret Wars*, Revised and Expanded Edition, Chicago: Ivan R. Dee, 1986.

Priest, Dana, and Bradley Graham, "Airstrikes Took a Toll on Saddam, U.S. Says," *Washington Post*, January 9, 1999.

Primakov, Yevgeni, "My Final Visit with Saddam Hussein," *Time*, March 11, 1991.

Prunckun, Henry W., Jr., *Operation El Dorado Canyon: A Military Solution to the Law Enforcement Problem of Terrorism: A*

Quantitative Analysis, dissertation, University of South Australia, Wayville, South Australia: Slezak Associates, 1994.

Public Records Office, *Operation Foxley: The British Plan to Kill Hitler*, Kew, U.K., 1998.

Rees, Matt, "The Work of Assassins," *Time*, January 15, 2001.

Reid, T. R., "British Spies Planned Many Deaths for Hitler," *Washington Post*, July 24, 1998.

Richburg, Keith B., "In War on Aideed, UN Battled Itself: Internal Conflict Stymied Decisions of Military Operations," *Washington Post*, December 6, 1993, p. 1.

Risen, James, "U.S. Welcomes Kurdish Leader Who Betrayed C.I.A. in Iraq," *New York Times*, July 25, 1998a.

_____, "Defining the Goal in Iraq," *New York Times*, December 23, 1998b.

_____, "How a Plot Convulsed Iran in '53 (and in '79)," *New York Times*, April 16, 2000.

Risen, James, and Barbara Crossette, "Even U.S. Sees Iraq Opposition as Faint Hope," *New York Times*, November 19, 1998.

Roosevelt, Kermit, *Countercoup: The Struggle for the Control of Iran*, New York: McGraw-Hill Book Company, 1979.

Rositzke, Harry, *CIA's Secret Operations*, New York: Reader's Digest Press, 1977.

Ross, Bruce A. (LCDR, USN), "The Case for Targeting Leadership in War," *Naval War College Review*, Winter 1993.

Sanger, David E., "The Plan: He Steps Down, They Step Up, U.S. Lies Low," *New York Times*, October 6, 2000, p. A15.

Schaffer, Ronald, *Wings of Judgment: American Bombing in World War II*, New York: Oxford University Press, 1985.

Schlesinger, Stephen, and Stephen Kinzer, *Bitter Fruit: The Untold Story of the American Coup in Guatemala*, New York: Doubleday & Company, Inc., 1982.

Schmemann, Serge, "Hit Parade: The Harsh Logic of Assassination," *New York Times*, Week in Review, October 12, 1997.

Schmitt, Michael N., "State-Sponsored Assassination in International and Domestic Law," *Yale Journal of International Law*, Vol. 17, Summer 1992.

Schumacher, Edward, "The United States and Libya," *Foreign Affairs*, Winter 1986/1987.

Schwarzkopf, H. Norman (GEN, USA, Ret.), *It Doesn't Take a Hero*, New York: Linda Grey Bantam Books, 1992.

Seenan, Gerald, "How the Trap Closed on the Libyan Bomber, *Guardian Weekly*, February 8–14, 2001.

Shenon, Philip, "U.S. General Warns of Dangers in Trying to Topple Iraq," *New York Times*, January 29, 1999.

Shultz, George P., *Turmoil and Triumph*, New York: Charles Scribner's Sons, 1993.

Shultz, Richard H., Jr., *The Secret War Against Hanoi: Kennedy and Johnson's Use of Spies, Saboteurs, and Covert Warriors in North Vietnam*, New York: HarperCollins, 1999.

Sieff, Martin, "New U.S. Game Plan to Oust Saddam Described," *Washington Times*, November 21, 1998.

Sims, Calvin, "On the Trail of Peru's Maoist Rebels," *New York Times*, August 8, 1996.

Smith, Joseph Burkholder, *Portrait of a Cold Warrior*, New York: G. P. Putnam's Sons, 1976.

Smith, Philip A. (Maj, USAF), *Bombing to Surrender: The Contributions of Airpower to the Collapse of Italy*, Maxwell Air Force Base, Ala.: Air University Press, August 1998.

Smith, R. Jeffrey, and Peter Finn, "How Milosevic Lost His Grip," *Washington Post*, October 15, 2000, pp. A1, A30.

Solarz, Stephen J., and Paul Wolfowitz, "How to Overthrow Saddam" (Letter to the Editor), *Foreign Affairs*, March/April 1999.

Sontag, Deborah, "Israel Acknowledges Hunting Down Arab Militants," *New York Times*, December 22, 2000.

_____, "Israel Hunts Down and Kills a Top Arafat Security Officer," *New York Times*, February 14, 2001.

Spector, Ronald H., *Eagle Against the Sun*, New York: The Free Press, 1985.

Stanik, Joseph T., *"Swift and Effective Retribution": The U.S. Sixth Fleet and the Confrontation with Qaddafi, The U.S. Navy in the Modern World Series*, No. 3, Washington, D.C.: Naval Historical Center, Department of the Navy, 1996.

Taylor, Philip M., *War and the Media: Propaganda and Persuasion in the Gulf War*, New York: Manchester University Press, 1992.

Thatcher, Margaret, *The Downing Street Years*, New York: HarperCollins, 1993.

Thomas, Evan, Christopher Dickey, and Gregory L. Vistica, "Bay of Pigs Redux," *Newsweek*, March 23, 1998.

Thurman, GEN Maxwell, former Commander-in-Chief, U.S. Southern Command, USAWC/USAMHI Senior Officer Oral History interview, Carlisle Barracks, Pa., Project No. 1992-1, 1992.

Tirpak, John A., "Deliberate Force," *Air Force*, Vol. 80, No. 10, October 1997.

Treverton, Gregory F., *Covert Action: The Limits of Intervention in the Postwar World*, New York: Basic Books, Inc., 1987.

"US Holding Talks on Financial Aid to Iraqi Opposition," *Agence France-Presse*, March 6, 2001. Online at http://asia.dailynews. yahoo.com/headline...n_financial_aid_to_Iraqi_opposition.html.

U.S. Department of the Air Force, *International Law: The Conduct of Armed Conflict and Air Operations*, AFP 110-31, Washington, D.C.: November 19, 1976.

U.S. Department of Defense, *Conduct of the Persian Gulf War: Final Report to Congress*, Washington, D.C.: U.S. Government Printing Office, April 1992.

U.S. Department of State, *Patterns of Global Terrorism: 1999*, Washington, D.C.: April 2000a. Online at http://www.state.gov/www/global/terrorism/1999report/eurasia.html (as of July 23, 2001).

_____, *Background Notes: Russia*, May 2000b.   Online at http://www.state.gov/www/background_notes/russia_0005_bgn. html (as of July 23, 2001).

_____, *Turkey—Consular Information Sheet*, October 2, 2000c. July 5, 2001 update online at http://travel.state.gov/turkey.html (as of July 23, 2001).

U.S. News & World Report, *Triumph Without Victory*, New York: Times Books, 1992.

U.S. Senate, *Alleged Assassination Plots Involving Foreign Leaders: An Interim Report of the Select Committee to Study Government Operations*, Washington, D.C.: U.S. Government Printing Office, 1975.

U.S. Special Operations Command, *Psychological Operations During Desert Shield/Storm: A Post-Operational Analysis*, 2nd ed., MacDill Air Force Base, Fla.: November 5, 1993.

U.S. Strategic Bombing Survey, *The Effects of Strategic Bombing on German Morale*, Vol. II, Washington, D.C., December 1946, in David MacIsaac, ed., *The United States Strategic Bombing Survey*, Vol. IV, New York: Garland Publishing, Inc., 1976.

United Nations, Security Council Resolution 837 (S/RES/837 1993), June 6, 1993.

Warner, Senator John and Senator Carl Levin, "Memorandum for Senator Thurmond and Senator Nunn," Washington, D.C.: U.S. Senate Committee on Armed Services, September 29, 1995.

Watts, Barry D., et al., *Gulf War Air Power Survey (GWAPS)*, Vol. II: *Operations and Effects and Effectiveness*, Part I: *Operations*, Washington, D.C.: U.S. Government Printing Office, 1993a.

_____, *Gulf War Air Power Survey (GWAPS), Volume II: Operations and Effects and Effectiveness, Part II: Effects and Effectiveness*, Washington, D.C.: U.S. Government Printing Office, 1993b.

Weiner, Tom, "Opponents Find That Ousting Hussein Is Easier Said Than Done," *New York Times*, November 16, 1998.

Wilber, Donald N., *CIA Clandestine Service History: Overthrow of Premier Mossadeq of Iran, November 1952–August 1953*, March 1954. Online at http://www.gwu.edu/~nsarchiv/NSAEBB/NSAEBB28/ (as of June 12, 2001).

Wyden, Peter, *Bay of Pigs*, New York: Simon and Schuster, 1979.

Zaman, Amberin, "Kurds' Surrender Awakens Turkish Doves," *Washington Post*, October 7, 1999.

Zengel, LCDR Patricia, "Assassination and the Law of Armed Conflict," *Military Law Review*, Fall 1991.

Ziemke, Earl F., *The U.S. Army in the Occupation of Germany 1944–1946*, Washington, D.C.: Center of Military History, United States Army, 1990.

Zimmermann, Tim, "Coercive Diplomacy and Libya," in Alexander L. George & William E. Simons, eds., *The Limits of Coercive Diplomacy*, Second Edition, Boulder, Colo.: Westview Press, 1994.